EVOLVED...

ENGAGING PEOPLE, ENHANCING SUCCESS

SURRENDERING OUR LEADERSHIP MYTHS AND RITUALS

GEORGE J. GARRETT &
THERESA M. ZIMMERMANN

WESTBOW°
PRESS
A DIVISION OF THOMAS NELSON
& ZONDERVAN

WestBow Press books may be ordered through booksellers or by contacting:

WestBow Press
A Division of Thomas Nelson & Zondervan
1663 Liberty Drive
Bloomington, IN 47403
www.westbowpress.com
1 (866) 928-1240

ISBN: 978-1-4908-5293-5 (sc)
ISBN: 978-1-4908-5329-1 (hc)
ISBN: 978-1-4908-5294-2 (e)

Library of Congress Control Number: 2014917185

Printed in the United States of America.

WestBow Press rev. date: 10/07/2014

Contents

Dedication

We affectionately thank George and Mable Garrett and Cyril and Donna Shircel, our parents, for providing us with a strong foundation of values. Without their love and guidance in our lives, we would have been unable to fulfill our passion for excellence.

We would be remiss if we did not acknowledge our spouses, Jeri Garrett and Ronald Zimmermann. Their unwavering support has allowed this book to happen.

We also thank those who played a part in our career paths. Whether recognized or not, many have been a part of our journey, and more than a few have been an inspiration to us.

Evolved

We all surrender, but not all surrender is honorable. If you surrender to the right things, surrender is not a sign of leadership weakness, but perhaps it is the ultimate sign of leadership confidence.

—Mike Myatt
N2Growth chairman and *Forbes Magazine* contributor

Introduction

> We are in one of those historical periods that occur every
> 200–300 years when people don't understand the world
> anymore, and the past is not sufficient to explain the future.
> —Peter Drucker

Leadership is in trouble.

One only has to look toward Washington, DC, to see how the lack of leadership impacts us all. With a divided government over the past several years, there is a great deal of finger-pointing from various sides, but no clear solutions. Laws are passed that don't make sense to the American people. Congress fights across the aisles and spirited, honorable debate is missing. Accusations, name-calling, and dirty tricks abound. Why? It seems politics have trumped statesmanship. Zero-sum games, where I win and you lose, seem everywhere. We seem divided rather than united.

The real losers in this game are the American people.

But it's not just Washington that has leadership issues. Over a decade since the first published report on employee engagement surfaced, engagement remains stagnant. There has been no change in this important dynamic for many years. Somewhere along the way, we have lost employees' desire to contribute to their organization. This lack of willingness affects society in general and individuals in particular. For example, absenteeism is almost 40 percent worse for organizations with disengaged employees. Turnover in less than engaged organizations is 60 percent worse. These are manageable costs, but we have accepted both too readily. And there are other costs too. Greater employee theft, poor safety performance, reduced quality, and overall profitability all factor into the equation.

Most unfortunately, when compared to the average in the world, the United States is a super power. The remainder of the world finds average employee engagement coming in at 13 percent. US employee engagement will be elaborated on throughout the book.

What a shame. What a waste.

Our research enabled us to look into the issues leadership, employee engagement, and motivation. After a very long and thoughtful process of deliberation, review of studies, and talking with individuals and groups, we concluded the key to all improvement invariably rests in the hands of leadership. Without leadership taking ownership of this, the outcomes of low workforce engagement will remain.

Leadership therefore must change. It must evolve.

But as Dr. Peter Drucker so clearly illustrated many years ago, times are confusing. In fact, some say it's worse now as a result of complexities that have accelerated. Global competition, the influx of social media in the workplace, diversity, and a host of other items have changed or are changing the way people interact with each other and the way they respond. Change and the associated confusion cause many to question what to do about it today, tomorrow, and well into the future.

The world has changed. But it appears leadership is stuck.

As a result, many leaders of today have their effectiveness and ability to lead questioned. There are numerous accusations which imply we face a leadership deficiency. Survey after survey support this general concept. More than a few polls indicate a vast number of workers are so dissatisfied that they are actively looking to leave their present employment. This is in spite of present economic uncertainty prevalent in both the United States and other parts of the world.

Based on myths, rituals and DNA, it appears leadership generally *is* failing the workers.

However, outcomes can be changed, starting now. Unlike disruptive technology, change is not necessarily quick, but it can be done in an orderly, transparent, and meaningful way. Changing behaviors and skill sets in conjunction with an eye toward improvement enables leaders to lead the change effort. This cannot be delegated. With the right approach and willingness to take ownership, a seemingly leadership crisis can be overcome. Practices and rituals that don't work any longer must be replaced with lasting and meaningful ones which transform the organization.

By instituting a system of modern leadership, a method that will work in private, government, for-profit organizations, and not-for-profit organizations will be realized. In other words, *all areas, all institutions, and all sectors* can benefit by instituting better guidance. New methods can be learned and poor leadership habits can be *un*learned. It starts with creating new practices and new behaviors which replace the old ones. It also means leadership must be willing loosen control—in essence, to surrender.

As this is being written, the US economy, crippled for the past several years, appears to be emerging from one of the most devastating economic periods since the beginning of the Great Depression. However, business cycles are exactly that: they are *cycles,* and once again, the United States will eventually enter a period of economic downturn. However, there are no leadership benchmarks such as found in economic cycles. Employee engagement has been deeply studied for the past decade and a half. The corresponding results are poor.

As the needs of the workforce evolve, so must leadership. What is needed is a future focus.

As you progress through the book, we encourage you to try a few new things, learn different approaches, and even revisit concepts learned in the past but shelved for whatever reason.

At the book's conclusion, you will have gained new knowledge. You will be able to utilize new techniques and methods designed to make you the leader of the future. These should have been a part of us long ago.

We invite you on a new leadership journey.

Chapter 1

The Leadership Conundrum

> If your actions inspire others to dream more, learn
> more, do more, and become more, you are a leader.
> —John Quincy Adams

Where we are today

It is an immutable fact that low employee-participation numbers
are weak, as indicated in articles, research, the blogosphere,
and various thought leaders concerning this important subject.
But these indicators are not new. They have been around for
some thirteen odd years and are at a virtual standstill. Some
may want to blame the new generation now entering the
workforce. Others may point to the near depression of 2009
to 2012.

Our thought is it's neither.

Looking back to the first reported employee engagement
numbers in 2000, the economy was essentially sound. Gross
domestic product was well over 3 percent and inflation was
low to moderate. Additionally, the newest generation of workers
was in grade school. They hardly can be blamed for such poor
results. So what are the dynamics that continue to drive such
low numbers?

Could it be practices are continued to be applied that don't fit the
workforce of today and tomorrow? Does the proverbial insanity
doctrine relate, meaning doing the same things over and over

again and expecting different results? If so, let's examine how we got to where we are today.

Our current method of producing goods and services was shaped by many people from the past. Some got it right; a few got it wrong. Unfortunately, we continue to believe the ones who got it wrong. With their associated incorrect theories, they negatively impacted us today. Rather than focusing on research that made sense, we, as leaders, followed the wrong trail. To understand leadership is to understand the many theories of motivation and management. Accordingly, the conduits which we consider to be the correct and just way are at odds with flawed methods that are still practiced in most US organizations today.

In the United States, there is little argument that we have been stellar at managing a business. However, it appears we have not had a great scorecard in terms of leadership. The sort of leadership that inspires people seems to have regressed.

Consider the following story.

A senior vice president of an international company asked one of his middle managers to accompany him to a business roundtable in New York City. John, the manager, asked what day the meeting was scheduled. When he was told, John informed the SVP he was supposed to be at a west-coast operation for another important meeting the very same day. The SVP told him it was extremely essential to accompany him to New York City, so John told him he would cancel his west-coast business trip. The SVP nixed that idea and said the west-coast trip was very important. In exasperation, John diplomatically told him it was impossible to be in two places at one time. He further asked the SVP what he wanted him to do. In a tremendous show of inspirational leadership, the SVP said, "Figure it out."

In this instance, there did not seem to be much leadership involved. Management control was prevalent, but certainly not leadership. The great patriot Thomas Paine once said, "Lead, follow, or get out of the way."

Warren Bennis, in *On Becoming a Leader,* illustrated it best. The following comparisons are stark. The roles of manager and leader are not necessarily parallel. This helps create the basis for understanding true leadership, especially now when it is needed most.

A Manager Manages ...	A Leader Leads ...
The manager administers.	The leader innovates.
The manager copies.	The leader is an original.
The manager maintains.	The leader develops.
The manager focuses on structure.	The leader focuses on people.
The manager relies on controls.	The leader inspires trust.
The manager has a short-range view.	The leader has a long-range perspective.
The manager's eye is on the bottom line.	The leader's eye is on the horizon.
The manager asks how and when.	The leader asks what and why.
The manager imitates.	The leader originates.
The manager accepts status quo.	The leader challenges it.
The manager does things right.	The leader does the right thing.

So what is leadership anyway?

There is a need for more leadership in the world. But what is leadership, anyway?

Leadership, like love, is a bit difficult to define. However, people instinctively know it when they see it or feel it. Historically, leadership has been defined as the ability to influence others while balancing management tasks with the human needs. Unfortunately, many of our so-called leaders today are really goal-centric tacticians and do not fall within the confines of the accepted definition. The causes of this are numerous and include the following key origins:

- <u>A short-term business focus</u>. A leader has to look on the edges, on the horizon as Warren Bennis states. Much too often though, leadership eyes the end of the month, end of the quarter, and so forth. People pick up on that and actually respond to it. Whatever message is given from the top cascades below. Admittedly, it is more and more difficult to perform longer-range planning due to technological upheavals. However, any organization that lives and breathes on a monthly or quarterly cycle cannot prepare for the future. Unfortunately, when leadership leads with a very short business focus, the focus usually is on the financial ends. Finance and money are important. We must cease relying on these as the sole data points and measures of success.
- <u>Global competition.</u> Some organizations don't think they compete in a global market. Think again. Competition from all corners of our world influence us in ways unheard a few short years ago. If leaders don't think in

global terms, they will eventually impact the organization negatively, even to the point of obsolescence.

- <u>Emphasis only on financial metrics.</u> This is equated to the first enumerated item, short-term focus. Think about financial metrics by themselves for a moment. Do they create a rallying cry, or do they appeal to greed? Studies have shown that an organization that does not act and behave in an altruistic sense will not be successful in the long term. We call it "money sickness" where the sole purpose is in the worship on the altar of capital. Generationally, this will cause problems down the road. Our newer generation of workers simply doesn't equate money as a factor of success. For example, in an article featured in the June 7, 2013 edition of the Houston Chronicle, ExxonMobil found they had trouble attracting younger operators for their chemical plants, even though pay for jobs of this sort, averaged $86,000 per year. Younger workers, according to the article, seemed to prefer working in a field where they could use their knowledge of technology rather than work in a job that was not attractive to them, even though the money was substantially less.

A person or organization who equates money with success is often wrong. History is rife with examples of a short-term focus creating superficial success. Google Enron.

Leadership is a skill that *can* be learned, should the leader want to embark on a journey to profound leadership. However, many leaders think they are doing the right thing when they are not. They have not learned how to lead, especially in a modern sense. Our past doesn't necessarily teach us anything, and styles learned a generation ago might not be applicable in today's world, much less in a future world.

One very important tenant of modern leadership is understanding the balance of process (how things work) and the people (who make things work). It is very common in many organizations to take care of issues ("Go kill something.") without understanding that all organizations are dependent on systems and processes in some way. Rather than attempting to comprehend these dynamics, too often, something is thrown against the wall in the hope of it sticking. Ordinarily, we don't just go out and buy a car without understanding the need, purpose, and usability. The same care and thought should go into business decisions, but many times, leaders rush into work solutions. We put something together in an organizational setting without understanding the very real unintended consequences of action. After all, isn't it the job of management to get things done?

Accordingly, the understanding of leadership is in need of an overhaul. It starts with understanding what motivates and calls people to action. It has a lot to do with leadership styles and ingrained DNA.

Motivation

To appreciate principles of leadership is to recognize the theories behind much of our motivational thinking, meaning what drives us and what makes us perform. There are four behaviorists who, in the twentieth century, either directly or indirectly influenced thinking on motivation. They are Abraham Maslow, Frederick Herzberg, Douglas McGregor, and B. F. Skinner.

Their impact continues to be felt long after their theories were first published and long after their deaths. Their background and theories must be understood for leadership to have appreciation for societal impact.

<u>Abraham Maslow (1908–1970).</u> Maslow was an American professor of psychology at Brandeis University, Brooklyn College, New School for Social Research, and Columbia University. He created Maslow's hierarchy of needs.

He stressed the importance of focusing on the positive qualities in people, as opposed to treating them as a bag of symptoms.

Maslow's most famous contributions center on the theory of hierarchy of needs (figure 1.1).

In short, his theory advocates that human beings satisfy needs in a hierarchal manner and after a need is satisfied they move on to the next one that needs fulfilling. These range from basic needs (food, shelter) to more advanced needs (self-esteem, respect). A normal human being under this theory cannot advance to the next level of need fulfillment until such time the preceding need is met, which then drives the pursuit of the next need. In simple terms, the human condition cannot meet an *esteem* need until a basic need, such as safety, security, employment, or health, is met.

From a motivational perspective, meaning things that drive us, this theory makes a great deal of sense and is easy to understand and apply.

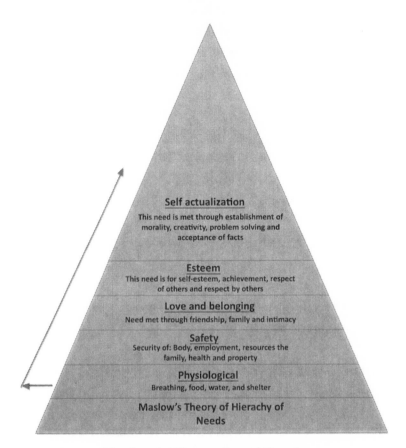

Maslow's Hierarchy of Needs

<u>Frederick Irving Herzberg (1923–2000).</u> Herzberg was an American psychologist who became one of the most influential names in business management. He is most famous for introducing job enrichment and the Motivation-Hygiene theory. His 1968 publication "One More Time: How Do You Motivate Employees?" had sold 1.2 million reprints by 1987 and was the most requested article from the *Harvard Business Review*.

Herzberg's two-factor theory is a bit more complex, but it helps explain the reasons behind the need for positive recognition and not relying on monetary factors as motivators.

His theory also touched on the effect rewards played on key motivators. His two-factor theory is found below and is separated by those factors that "motivate" us and those factors that become *expected* or simply hygienic.

Motivating Factors	Hygiene Factors
<ul><li>achievement</li><li>recognition</li><li>work itself</li><li>responsibility</li><li>promotion</li><li>growth</li></ul>	<ul><li>pay and benefits</li><li>company policy and administration</li><li>relationship with coworkers</li><li>supervision</li></ul>

It must be pointed out that hygiene needs are cyclical in nature and come back to a starting point. This leads to the "What have you done for me lately?" question and creates an escalating zero point and no final answer.

Herzberg's theory presumed that *money* is not a motivator except for the completion of very short-term results. However, in the absence of hygiene factors, such as money, relationships, and good supervision, they have a tendency to *de-motivate* people.

His theory was widely taught in business schools and created a need for management and leadership to place more emphasis on "recognizing" employees, thus the advent of employee-recognition systems along with understanding that pay and benefits *do not* necessarily motivate people to do their best.

Douglas Murray McGregor (1906–1964). Macgregor was a management professor at the MIT Sloan School of Management and president of Antioch College. He also taught at the Indian Institute of Management Calcutta.

His 1960 book *The Human Side of Enterprise* had a profound influence on education practices. In the book, he identified an approach of creating an environment which employees are motivated via authoritative, direction, and control versus integration and self-control, which he called theory X and theory Y, respectively.

Theory Y is the practical application of Dr. Abraham Maslow's Humanistic School of Psychology, applied to scientific management. Unfortunately, McGregor's Theory X and Theory Y have been misunderstood and misinterpreted over time. The following illustrates assumptions on both theories and are not complete but show the unambiguous contrast between both sets of assumptions.

Theory X	Theory Y
Most people dislike work and will avoid it if they can.	The expenditure of physical and mental work is as natural as work or play.
Humans like to be directed and desire security above all else.	Humans will direct themselves if committed to the aims of an organization.
The average human dislikes responsibility and will also avoid it.	If a job is satisfying, the result will be commitment to the organization.
Humans must be controlled and threatened before they will work hard enough.	Average people, under proper conditions, will seek out responsibility.

McGregor argued that the conventional approach to managing was based on three major propositions, which he called Theory X.

1. Management is responsible for organizing the elements of productive enterprise—money, materials, equipment, and people—in the interests of economic ends.
2. With respect to people, this is a process of directing their efforts, motivating them, controlling their actions, and modifying their behavior to fit the needs of the organization.
3. Without this *active* intervention by management, people would be passive—even resistant—to organizational needs. They must therefore be persuaded, rewarded, punished, and controlled. Their activities must be directed. Management's task was thus simply getting things done through other people.

McGregor put forth the following Theory Y assumptions, which he believed could lead to more *effective* management of people in the organization. The major propositions of Theory Y include diametrically opposed Theory X beliefs, with the exception of management's organizing requirements.

1. Management continues to be responsible for organizing the elements of productive enterprise, such as money, materials, equipment, and people, in the interests of achieving economic ends.
2. People are not by nature passive or resistant to organizational needs. They have become so as a result of experience in organizations.
3. The motivation, potential for development, capacity for assuming responsibility, and readiness to direct behavior toward organizational goals are all present in people.

Management does not put them there. It is a responsibility of management to make it possible for people to recognize and develop these human characteristics for themselves.

4. The essential task of management is to arrange organizational conditions and methods of operation so that people can achieve their own goals by directing their efforts toward organizational objectives.

Even though McGregor never intended Theory X to be a model of motivation, schools taught there are times Theory X needed to be applied. This is misunderstood. However, he clearly outlined what we know as "carrots and sticks" that continue to be used to motivate employees.

B. F. Skinner (1904–1990). B. F. Skinner was an American behaviorist, author, inventor, social philosopher, and poet. He was the Edgar Pierce Professor of Psychology at Harvard University from 1958 until his retirement in 1974. He is known as the father of operant conditioning.

Skinner's writings and teachings have infiltrated the workplace, yet many leaders may never have heard of him. Peter Scholtes, noted business psychologist, summed it best when he wrote that organizations of today (schools and workplaces) have incorporated Skinner teachings. Scholtes complained that the Skinner methods of human behavior is a set of responses that can be conditioned, just as owners of pets train their animals to behave in certain ways with combinations of rewards and punishment, thus the birth of performance appraisal.

Skinner's teachings gave rise to what we consider an unproductive management ritual. Performance appraisal is a manner of reward and punishment, winners and losers. The odd thing about Skinner's research is he did most of the research on pigeons, took the results, and applied them to people.

It's no wonder why people generally dislike performance appraisals. In fact, upward of 98 percent of employees despise them.

Of all the twentieth-century behaviorists, B. F. Skinner took prominence. His operant conditioning theory prevailed. Why? We believe educators latched on to his theory and it was taught in schools, which is why today it is the prevalent manner we utilize to motivate the workforce. Perhaps it was easy, too easy. After all you do right, and you are rewarded. You do wrong, and you are punished.

Unfortunately, concepts like operant conditioning have been proven ineffective in the long term and simply do not work. Yet we continue to incentivize people and place them into some form of regimented performance appraisal process. These have become part of our leadership DNA.

When challenged on the usefulness of these concepts, both management and leadership have a tendency to look at the challenger as if they had a third eye growing in the middle of their forehead. Skinner's teachings have become pervasive and common in the workplace.

As W. Edwards Deming said, "All theories are right in some world."

Leadership Traits

As previously mentioned, the term *leadership* has been bandied around for many years, but there is no clear definition or even a consistent explanation for what a leader is. This may be due to our attempt to establish a one-size-fits-all description of a leader.

It's not that simple.

Often, when asked to define leadership, people respond, "I can't describe it, but I know it when I see it." This is perhaps due to there being no one singular way to lead. However, going back to the accepted definition of leadership, that being *the ability to influence others while balancing management tasks with the human needs,* we will have established at least an understanding of what sound leadership is.

There is a minimum of ten fundamental traits leaders must possess to be effective in a modern sense. The following list encompasses the ideal characteristics that become the competencies associated with good leadership. These competencies will help us on our journey toward profound leadership. They are all interrelated in every respect.

- self-assessment
- resiliency
- interpersonal and leadership skills
- communications skills
- employee development (coaching and inspiring)
- customer orientation
- strategic business acumen
- project leadership
- creating and actualizing vision
- create, support and manage change

Self-Assessment

How difficult is it to perform an internal assessment of ourselves? Without some guideposts, it may be rather vexing. Let's start with understanding ourselves. First, a leader needs to be excellent at developing clarity. This means developing clarity of personal values and clarity of their own purpose and mission.

Ask yourself the following questions:

1. What things, ideas, or values do I cherish the most?
2. How do I know these are valued by me?
3. How do I inform people of these? What signals do I provide so people know I am sincere about my personal values?

These sorts of questions also help when questioning the task, goal, or strategy.

People have a quick judgment of people who say one thing and then go out and perform tasks opposite of the stated values. Once this is done, it is difficult to reverse course as people get branded more by their actions and deeds than their words.

This requires a leader to demonstrate *authenticity* through behavioral alignment with values and vision. These will be explored later on in the chapter on finding purpose and leads to accountability for personal and leadership actions.

A leader who "passes the buck," fails to hold personal accountability, and blames others will create fear that will infiltrate the workplace. This will ultimately undermine the organization, as the shadow of leadership is truly pervasive.

Resiliency

Too often, once a leader is established, they have a tendency to think there is no room for further training, education, or self-improvement. How many times have you seen top leadership expect attendance at training sessions but exempt themselves?

Modern leadership requires a willingness to step in and get things started. However, this is not meant in a sense they must do *everything.* Sound principles of delegation and managing must still surround this important leadership competency. This means providing a basis for empowering people to do their best. It also means it is acceptable for the leader to be clumsy and not totally knowledgeable. It is really acceptable to not know everything.

Case in point, a little over a hundred years ago, major technological changes occurred on an average of once every two to three generations. Today major technological changes occur continuously.

Who can discern everything in today's hyper-drive world? It's virtually impossible.

Leaders must persist though, even when things do not work well the first time. There are myriad examples of persistence. Thomas Edison encountered one thousand failures before he invented the light bulb. Leaders must take a proactive stance by seeking new ideas, new opportunities, new markets, new products, and new services.

Interpersonal and Relationship Skills

There was a time when groupthink was the norm and it just wasn't correct to disagree with the boss. The boss was the boss because he or she knew everything there was to know about any given operation. What a difference a generation makes! Now it is common for people to express themselves and even disagree with an opinion, because it is just an opinion and not fact.

Thus, diversity was born.

Today, we live in a very diverse society. Over time, the barriers based on race, religion, color, or sex have become less obvious and are not accepted in the business world. Different genders and ethnicities have allowed us to travel beyond our internal borders and expand our horizons. Ask yourself, "What is diversity, and why is it a factor in the leader possessing interpersonal and relationship skills?"

Communication Skills

How and when we communicate often determines the success or failure of organizations. First examine a pathway that standard communications follows.

Good communication requires as much planning and coordination as other aspects of the business. The following illustration helps understand the path communications takes, even when designed with the best intentions.

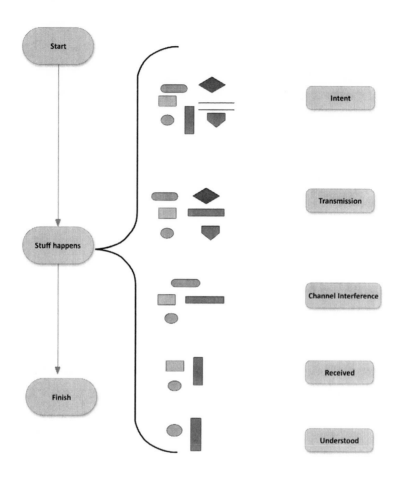

In this example, the initiator of the communication has in their mind a message to send. These are represented by the seven different symbols. As the transmission begins, things become a bit unclear. When channel interference occurs, the original message intent is down to 57 percent. When the message is received, the intent drops to 42 percent. Finally, as understood by the recipient, only 29 percent of the original message remains.

With a global slant today, communications becomes even more important to the health and long-term welfare of any organization.

Employee Development (Coaching and Inspiring)

A key aspect that is undergoing metamorphosis today surrounds employee development. In the past, a good leader was required to motivate employees. "Reward them for good behavior, and punish them for poor behavior" was the mantra leaders lived by.

New science is quickly debunking this "myth" and proving carrots and sticks no longer work in a hyper-connected world.

Unfortunately, the teachings of B. F. Skinner infiltrated the workplace and have been around for generations. His teachings and institutional acceptance created a real leadership conundrum. The educational system taught leaders of today as well as the future the importance of motivating employees. To put it mildly, the techniques have proven to not work in today's world (or maybe never have). Today, the leader must coach rather than motivate and inspire people for improvement. They also must utilize respect of the need for diversity, values, and individuality.

Also, proper delegation must be used, with delegation done in the right way, not merely giving a person an order. Autonomy and freedom to perform are the new delegation concepts in today's world and tomorrow's world. Going forward, autonomy is going to be the new driver of employee involvement. The leader will become more of a coach and much less authoritative to accomplish this.

Customer Orientation

A better understanding of the chain of events that surround the concept of the customer is found when understanding and applying systems. Previously, and under the old paradigm, customers were viewed as complete outsiders to the organization. In fact, much research was devoted to determining customer needs and then tailoring a product or service to fit those needs.

Then along came Steve Jobs and Apple computers. Apple did not believe in customer research or even customer-focus groups. Apple created customer needs yet paid attention to customers by ever improving its products and services to simplify the product experience. It changed the way the world uses computing, music, and communications. However, it listened to customers when products did not meet key expectations and made improvements to retain their loyalty. Today, Apple is one of the world's richest and most stable companies. It retains customers by offering them a rewarding, easy experience. Apple customers are, above all else, *loyal.*

Strategic Business Acumen

There was an old axiom that for-profit companies were in the business to make money. While that is an outcome, it can no longer be the sole focus of *any* organization. Today, customers and employees want and demand something more altruistic. To be straightforward, if the sole driver of an organization is to make money, many of them may be in the wrong business. After all, running guns and illegal drugs are both quite lucrative businesses.

Challenges today require leaders to demonstrate the ability to ethically build and support perspectives for which the organization feels strongly about. This requires greater emphasis on systems as well as the effects and consequences of actions and decisions. Research Enron and Bernie Madoff. Both are examples of filtering out the consequences of actions and behaviors.

Leaders of today must operate with awareness of marketplace competition and the general landscape of related business arenas. There is no substitute for a leader effectively doing the right thing. A leader who thinks and acts strategically in areas of planning, finance, marketing, manufacturing, and R&D enables his or her organization to behave in an ethical, long-term, financially healthy environment.

There is no room for taking shortcuts which cause loss of bearings and direction.

Project Leadership

Let's face it. In today's world, we all manage teams, be it natural work teams or project teams. This requires project leadership that helps foster commitment and desire from employees. Leader's must set, communicate, and monitor milestones and stumbling blocks on the pathway to success. This requires the leader to gain buy-in and maintain it from many areas of the organization and even outside the organization, relating to external customers.

The modern leader understands, prioritizes, and allocates resources and many times manages multiple, even conflicting, priorities across many diverse disciplines. The ability to project-manage thus becomes key to organizational success. Leaders must interact and foster a productive team culture and manage the process throughout its life cycle.

Creating and Actualizing Vision

One of the more difficult aspects of leadership is creating and actualizing the vision of the organization. Returning to Steve Jobs and Apple as a benchmark, Jobs wanted to create a stylish, enjoyable, fully integrated customer experience in its products and services. If nothing else, Steve Jobs was a visionary. The iPod, iPad, and iPhone are the standards in which competitors measure and relate.

Today, creating a clear and inspirational vision of a desired outcome is vital. It requires aligning the vision with broader organizational strategies and then translating the vision into manageable steps used to achieve it.

Above all, vision is facilitating a win-win solution. No longer should zero-sum game attitudes prevail, be it in the workplace or Washington, DC. The institution will eventually fail if allowed to continue this trajectory.

Creating, Supporting, and Managing Change

Finally, one of the most important characteristics modern leadership must possess is the ability to create, support, and manage change. Change is all around us; it's constant. As technology pervades more and more into organizations and affects our communications, leadership must be ready *and* responsive. The next disruptive change is around the corner. Change will continue, even more rapidly. Leaders can either be ready for it or be victims of it.

When you think about it, there are probably only two states any organization exists in: the ones moving forward or the ones moving backward. Remaining stationary is no longer an option. Static, most likely, will disappear.

Accordingly, to create, support, and manage change requires that the leader understands three improvement initiatives/levels.

1. Leaders must manage their own transition and transformation.
2. Leaders must be able to manage a change initiative.
3. Leaders must know how to coach others through the transition.

Using vision and strategy, the modern leader will identify and implement appropriate change initiatives and efforts and even promote and build support for the change advantages. Of course, they will need to understand and utilize cost/benefit and ROI regarding change efforts. Change without improvement is waste.

Leaders must also manage these transition with employees and guide and support the change process. Change is often murky at times, and the leader will support staff in navigating the transitional process and many challenges that accompany organizational change. Leaders consistently demonstrate and build *resilience* in the face of change.

The old competencies required leadership to possess the following attributes, which no longer work in a modern sense. The new, modern leader will need to overcome these old competency models:

- forceful and in control
- motivating
- assertive

- results oriented
- task oriented
- honest, diplomatic

So in the twenty-first century, do these attributes fit? Perhaps the honesty attribute, but not the others.

Today and beyond require a more robust manner of leading. As the workforce changes, we simply cannot subscribe to the old style of leadership. In fact, the future workforce will need and even demand a leadership that embodies the principles found in Maslow, Herzberg, and McGregor. A modern workforce should dismiss the concepts and principles promoted by Skinner. Skinner's teachings do not fit the modern society of today or the world of the future. The enlightened leader must adapt to a new way.

This requires them to be more coach than boss.

The Leader as a Coach

Marcus Buckingham, coauthor of the best-selling book *First, Break All the Rules*, wrote, "The corporate world is appallingly bad at capitalizing on the strength of its people." This is so true. He was directing his rebuke at leaders who appear to be ill equipped and even unwilling to capture the energy of people and enlisting them to achieve corporate goals. This lack of engagement by leaders denigrates into lack of engagement by the people of the organization.

A case can be made for instituting a strong and vibrant workforce in which leaders engage the "hearts and minds" of the individuals, including teams to harness the talents that contribute to high-performance results. Coaching, rather than command and control techniques, fulfills the need that Mr. Buckingham illustrates so well. The following are key characteristics of the leader as a coach.

First and foremost, they are excellent listeners. They hear and understand what their clients say and respect what they say. They also possess solid business acumen. They understand the business and look toward the things that truly matter in the organization.

They also possess solid ethics and personal values. These are translated into behaviors that are followed day in and day out. Accordingly, they have a high level of emotional intelligence, which enables them to understand and work through complexities. Furthermore, they hold themselves and others accountable for actions, but not in the way that punishes mistakes. They understand we are all humans and work to coach them to a better and more productive way of handling issues.

Of course, they are also results oriented, but not in the manner where one is made to feel inferior whenever mistakes are made. The modern leader creates those teachable moments where all can learn. Also, they are visionary. They create a clearly defined vision of the future and embrace life-long learning.

Finally, they are optimists and experts at developing lasting, meaningful relationships.

In days past, a leader needed to be counted on to swing for the fences in everything they touched. In today's competitive world, more is less. Leaders do not have to feel inadequate if they don't necessarily have all the answers. There is purely too much knowledge and too much information available to adequately keep up with.

In the past, traditional leaders felt the following attributes were the litmus test for effectiveness. You will note many of these are steeped in *fear* as a driver.

- feeling that you have to be the expert and have all the answers
- fear of being vulnerable to others
- impatience with other people's pace of change
- continually connecting coaching to performance appraisal
- underestimating other people's abilities
- expecting the individual to change first and prior to effecting other forms of change
- expecting coaching to be a "quick fix"
- losing control

Rather than improving leadership, the attributes listed above turned the leader into a manager of outcomes. A better way is using leadership to coach for performance. Coaching requires a much different level of skill to be an effective coordinator of people, systems, and teams.

Today, it is more important for the modern leader to have the ability to ask the right questions, rather than be expected to have all the answers.

To help reinforce this concept, management is compared to coaching. Thus, coaching is very aligned with true leadership when compared to the Warren Bennis model.

Managing v. Coaching

A Manager Behaves This Way.	A Coach Behaves This Way.
based on position of power	based on relationships and influence
directive, provides solutions	facilitative and uses participative methods
reactive to situations and behavior	takes a proactive approach before issues arise
works from a command and control perspective	encourages inclusion and engagement in decision making
accepts "meets expectations" results	expects high performance from everyone
accepts the status quo	willing to "rock the boat" and be visionary
bases decisions on history and own knowledge	open to new learning
looks to policies and procedures to find answers	asks others for potential solutions
works toward incremental improvements	looks for breakthrough improvements
is not inclusive in decision making	uses questions in discussing problems

Susan Wright, a distinguished author and coach, writes, "Unfortunately, most corporate leaders are not good coaches." She illustrates that coaching requires a certain level of emotional intelligence that normally makes people feel *uncomfortable.* Her point is that leaders have to let go of their technical side of involvement and concentrate on personal *and* interpersonal skill to achieve the sort of results desired by most organizations.

This includes those "soft" skills of managing performance, giving feedback, confronting issues, dealing with conflict, and many other things that are outside our comfort zone.

A leader must rebalance things and develop competencies pertaining to external factors, such as strategy, priorities, and results, combined with values, purpose, and awareness of self.

Thus, the leader as a coach requires abilities to

- demonstrate commitment to their own development and learning
- promote inclusiveness by involving others in solving problems
- inspire others by having a vision for themselves *and* the organization
- encourage others to continually learn
- promote better solutions by engaging everyone and increasing potential solutions

The following is a cycle of coaching that can be universally adopted by organizations. Note that it begins with recognizing an issue exists. Honing in on the issue becomes the basic tenet of coaching individuals. It must be clear, and it requires a mutual understanding of the issue before moving forward with solutions.

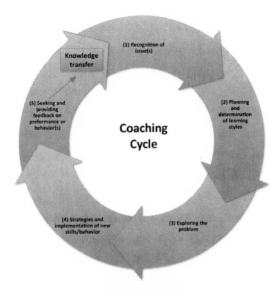

Coaching Cycle

This clearly eliminates a need to swing for the fences.

Thus far, we have explored where we are today and some explanations for how we wound up in a leadership conundrum. There was an exploration of modern leadership traits along with differences in managing v. leadership and coaching.

The following is an example of leadership. You be the judge of its effectiveness.

The employee had commendations in his file. He was well respected by his peers and management for his overall enthusiasm, commitment, and service. However, his home life was in shambles. In spite of this, he continued to deliver quality work day in and day out.

One evening, however, things took a turn. With his marital problems mounting and looking for consolation, he needed to talk to a friend privately. He found an unattended office with a telephone and decided to make a personal call on his lunch break.

It so happened that a security guard making rounds saw a small light on in an office that was not occupied, so he investigated. When the guard opened the door and turned all the lights on, he found the employee crouched down and trying to hide with the phone in his hand.

The next business day, management was made aware of this incident. In the eyes of the operations manager, this was a severe violation of protocol so he gave an order to terminate employment of this twelve-year, loyal, and dedicated employee. Of course, the operations manager's subordinates found this action to be rather harsh, so they appealed the decision to him. The operations manager could not be convinced, even though the employee's record was "commendable" and even though his peers, his supervisor, and human resources thought a termination was simply unjustified in this case. Surely, a terse final warning was more in line, especially given the employee's overall service record.

The operations manager was adamant. His order was followed, in spite of reasons supporting mitigation. The employee was called in and terminated. The employee freely admitted to being in the wrong and literally begged for his job to be saved.

The employee drove home to his wife and explained what happened. The situation escalated into a brawl. In anger he shot his wife dead. He then walked to the police station and turned himself in.

Two lives were lost that day.

The preceding story is very unsettling. Had leadership been willing to mitigate things, a tragedy may have been avoided.

We need better leadership. We need a system of leadership which provides a clear pathway for today and well into the future. We will explore a much different model at the end of this book. The model reflects what is important in today's world and the world beyond.

Chapter 2

Myths, Rituals, and DNA:
The Need for Profound Leadership

> You are what you do, not what you say you'll do.
> —Carl Jung

As with most things in life, organizations and leadership are evolving. Unfortunately, our past way of leading will not propel us forward.

Over the past sixty or so years, we have developed some leadership habits that don't fit in a more modernistic world. Along the way, we developed several rituals, with some steeped in myth, that run counter to how people learn, how people grow, and how people are motivated. In spite of things articulated by McGregor, Herzberg, Maslow, we chose to follow the lead of B. F. Skinner, who expounded and promoted a carrots and stick approach.

As we get further into the twenty-first century, his teachings are basically becoming mythical, yet ritualistic enough to be difficult habits to break.

Leadership Myths

Leadership is oftentimes embroiled with issues regarding what things motivate, guide, and improve people. This is in spite of what we know about the human condition. We have taken our natural curiosity and willingness to do the right thing and, rather than encouraging these, spent considerable effort and time trying to motivate people. We have forgotten that the best motivation comes from within. External motivation leans toward fear.

Here is the quandary of this and many more things. If employees aren't motivated, then should we look to their leaders and organizational practices as a cause of this?

We believe organizations have failed people's innate desire to achieve by replacing it with artificial inducements to do well. Here are several myths and rituals that have become a part of our leadership DNA. These must be changed if organizations want to avoid the brewing tsunami that is about to hit us. Let's start with a practice that has long outlived its usefulness and utility.

The dreaded performance appraisal and processes associated with this old ritual damages so many people year in and year out.

❶ Performance appraisal: your check, my neck.

First, do your employees believe their maximum efforts will be recognized in performance appraisals? For many employees, the response is a resounding no. Their skill level may be deficient, which means that no matter how hard they try, they're unlikely to be high performers. The following question has been asked in various group sizes, ranging from the very small (less than ten) to the very large (two hundred plus): "Do you like the concept of performance appraisal?" In a large group setting, there have been moans and groans, and in the smaller setting, the preponderance of the people resoundingly said no!

Solicited feedback is supported by various surveys, which clearly shows the futility of the process.

- 98 percent of employees dread them as reported in various surveys.
- 14 percent of employers don't even have them.
- 12 percent of employees don't receive feedback from them, even when they are used.
- More than 50 percent of employees who undergo the process and receive evaluations believe the results are not fair or accurate.

So why do we continue this practice?

There are several myths to explore tucked inside the concept of performance appraisal, starting with what Peter Scholtes described as faults common to all forms of performance appraisal (PA).

PA Myth 1. Appraisal works.

This is false. Appraisal simply does not work. In fact, no research is able to demonstrate that any organization is improved by the use of performance appraisal. Dr. Scholtes even went as far as to explain that any research conducted on performance appraisal involved using a sample from the groups that espouse it in the first place. This means research is performed on consulting companies which teach it or human resources practitioners who implement and monitor it. In other words, the research is flawed.

It is believed that over 90 percent of all appraisal systems are not successful. When we see the indicators from the people we poll, the percent of unsuccessful systems seems so much higher.

PA Myth 2. Appraisal targets those in need of help.

This is another falsehood. One does not need to be judged on an annual or semiannual basis and targeted for help. What has been instilled in us is the belief that if we don't have a record of this, various courts, and especially lawyers, will seize upon this and the organization will be punished. Doesn't this form of documentation induce fear? At a minimum, it places an employee under a microscope for further evaluation of actions, very similar to a medical researcher trying to isolate a new microbe.

PA Myth 3. Appraisal is a form of feedback.

Let's be frank. Appraisal is a form of judgment. Period. Consider the following firsthand scenario. It involves someone who casually mentioned he had received his annual performance appraisal. He works in a technical field. This person is very particular about his work. He is very involved in delivering a superior service.

> "Hey, I had my performance evaluation today. My boss tells me he loves assigning things to me because he knows they will be done right, he and everyone else loves working with me, and he doesn't know what he would do without me. A sigh of relief was at hand because there appeared to be no gotcha moments."

But then he goes on to say, "My boss said that if he had to say anything bad, he would say that my work is too perfect!"

The dreaded performance appraisal has claimed yet another victim. Except in this particular case, the employee doesn't even know the process zeroed in on a negative, which in reality is not a negative in the least bit.

Think about it. Your work is too perfect? Isn't perfection a desirable attribute? So a perfect performance appraisal is not so perfect after all.

Linking Pay and Performance

Many companies have tried for a very long time to link pay and performance. This is done by dangling money in front of people (like a carrot in front of a mule). A meeting is conducted and the boss goes over strengths and weaknesses. At the end, depending on what he or she feels about the performance, the raise or bonus is then calculated. Valid research has conclusively found that performance reviews tied into compensation schemes create an excuse-driven culture. Dr. Peter Scholtes wrote that this type of scenario is the one time a year you absolutely know who has domain over you.

Performance appraisal that ties into compensation creates hierarchy and works against problem resolution and problem solving. It ultimately derails our intrinsic motivation. It's demoralizing to all people, even the high performer. After all, he or she will be demoralized once they reach the top of the range. Once achieving this distinction, there is a reality they will eventually reach a point where future raises are minimized, if given at all. This doesn't seem to be a very noteworthy exercise.

What really transpires is an ineffective system whereby people fight over scraps with competition intensifying as an employee fights for a half percent more than the other person, based on the final evaluation.

Really? Is this the signal as leaders we want to send to workers? The result is pitting people against people. This is detrimental to any efforts aimed at instilling engagement.

This leads to an inevitable question: how do we reward people if not through a formalized process such as performance appraisal? There are many better ways to do this. Here is just one.

> In the United States, free markets dictate prices. Why not apply this to pay? Market-based pay, be it local, regional, or national helps alleviate any association between performance and pay. Previous and highly respected behaviorists from generations ago proved money is not a motivator. Why continue this practice? Why use performance appraisal as a method to derive pay?

Performance appraisal is judgment of one human being to another. So once again, there is little evidence to support employing a practice that doesn't work, never has, and probably never will. It's most likely due to it being part of our DNA. And our DNA needs altering if we are going to lead in the twenty-first century.

❷ We need to motivate employees.

Another leadership myth we engage in day in and day out is the premise that people simply lack the motivation to work. Accordingly, they need to be prodded, held accountable, enlightened and made to follow certain rules, all of which are designed to make for a healthier, more productive workforce.

We find ways to reward contributors and, when required, do the flip side of reward: punishment. Carrots and sticks make for peace and harmony in the workplace.

We have been "Skinnered" into believing this.

Looking at what Maslow, Herzberg, and McGregor attempted to teach industry, the practice of rewards and punishment simply would not be needed in the work setting. So the question is this: do we need to motivate the workforce? Let's dig deeper into the idea of motivation.

Perhaps it has a beginning we fail to recognize and factor into why the belief of motivating the workforce exists. Its beginning may have started well over one hundred years ago at the dawning of our own industrial revolution. There was one man who observed the waste associated with lack of efficiency. His name is Frederick W. Taylor.

As people moved from farms to work in factories in the early 1900s, and the industrial complex was being developed, Taylor, an engineer, found that factories operated in a highly inefficient manner. He invented a method called scientific management. This method equated people to parts of a machine, and if they did their work in the right way, at the right time, the entire machine would function smoothly. To do this, management rewarded the behavior that was sought and punished the behavior that was discouraged. The thinking was that if you did this, people would respond rationally to this sort of extrinsic motivation. This method was quickly adapted throughout all of industry.

Today it is so deeply imbedded in our lives that we don't even realize it is present. Face time, logical order of jobs, and efficiency pervade the business world. The way to improve performance, increase productivity, and encourage excellence is to reward the good and punish the bad. In a way, people were no different from the way we train animals. But there can be no doubt this system worked very well ... until it didn't, and certainly not in the modern sense today.

Then in the 1940s, B. F. Skinner expounded and promoted the concept of operant conditioning, where a series of rewards and punishment sought to improve the concept derived from Taylor.

B. F. Skinner was a true believer of rewards and punishment and incorporated the concept of carrots and sticks. The new science of operant conditioning made sense to both industry and educational institutions. He felt the key to motivating a workforce lay in the tenets where one rewards good behavior and punishes or withholds rewards for poor behavior. Just like is done in the performance appraisal.

However, humans have higher drives than those of the animal world. What happened, which allowed this to infiltrate the industrial world, is academia accepted his ideas wholeheartedly. Educators taught generation upon generation the need for reward and punishment. These teachings continue today. Accordingly, in leadership's attempt to motivate the workforce, performance appraisal and the outlier called incentives infiltrate most organizations today.

Many people believe the methods work when, in actuality, they don't. Unfortunately, performance appraisal used to motivate along with incentive plans have been a difficult concept to dispel in most organizations. This has been difficult to dislodge. Whenever these misguided concepts are explained to leadership, there is tremendous pushback. Leadership has been instilled in this form of teaching. To something contrary to what was taught would be viewed as an alien arriving from a different solar system.

So why doesn't this work? This is the basis of the next myth.

❸ Incentives work.

Money is *not* a motivator. That is, unless one is motivated by greed. Once again, most human beings have a higher drive than those dictated by greed. However, there are a few who taint this motivational theory.

Frederick Herzberg wrote extensively about motivation and developed the two-factor theory regarding it. Too bad previous generations of managers and leaders didn't heed what he said. He was one of the first to articulate that *money* is not a motivator. What motivates us to do more, work harder, and produce more are

- achievement
- recognition
- work itself
- responsibility

- promotion
- growth

With respect to money? Herzberg said it's like company policy and administration, supervision and benefits. Just something that is there but will not drive us higher (except for greed). However, whenever there is an absence of money, meaning below a certain standard, the natural inclination is to be demotivated. Hence, leadership should pay a proper amount. However, paying more will simply not motivate most of us to do more.

So why do leaders insist on incentivizing people, given the tried and true theories of motivation? Is this fallout from capitalism or do managers think it truly works? We believe things are easily corrupted once money is used as an inducement.

According to Wharton Speaks, financial incentives played a very large role in the near collapse of the economy in 2008 and 2009. In a micro sense, incentives also hamper ability to do the right thing. Again, a greed factor may emerge once incentives are placed in the motivational mix of things.

An example of this follows.

> Some time ago, a major consumer packaged goods company experienced a huge problem at one of its plants: frozen peas were somehow being packaged with insect parts. Management hoped to improve this quality issue by designing an incentive program whereby employees received a bonus for finding insect parts.

> Employees responded in grand fashion. They began bringing insect parts from home. They planted them in

frozen pea packages and then discovered them to earn the bonus.

Incentivizing did not achieve the desired results. The solution using money as a motivator created unintended greed.

Too often, when financial incentives are put in place, people will cross the ethical divide in order to earn the incentive. Many times, we value a reward to the extent that we will take the shortest, easiest path to obtain it, all the while trying to rationalize that no harm was really done.

Other times, financial incentives create unhealthy internal competition, whereby silos are formed. Rather than enhancing a spirit of teamwork, silos are established, which may create confusion, infighting, and pay issues. In fact, studies have shown that organizations with greater disparity in pay encounter greater manager and employee turnover. This doesn't happen in just the traditional for-profit type organizations either. It even cuts to the sports realm. The same studies point to problems with baseball teams that have larger pay gaps between highest and lowest paid players also lose more games, score fewer runs, and allow more runs scored. This correlation does not exist in teams where pay was more evenly compressed. This creates a fairness (or unfairness) issue, which sabotages overall efforts.

In recent years, the public has gotten involved with people representing the 99 percent of workers railing against the top 1 percent of earners. Something is truly amiss whenever the typical US CEO earns substantially more than the average worker. This will be discussed further in another chapter, but the point is pronounced power and influence requires great responsibility for people and society.

In recent times, even with increased CEO spending, things have not materially improved in most organizations. This will be also be explored further.

In the meantime, and once again, financial incentives produce undesired results and do nothing to motivate people.

❹ We need control.

For those who remember March 31, 1980, an assassination attempt was made on President Ronald Reagan. A great deal of confusion ensued. Vice President George H. W. Bush was not in town, which is the normal line of succession, both temporarily and permanently. General Alexander Haig, Reagan's secretary of state, took to a White House briefing and said the constitutional line of succession was the president, vice president, and secretary of state. He was wrong. Third in line is the speaker of the House of Representatives. Based on his own misunderstanding of lines of succession, he uttered those now famous words "I am in control here."

Management and control of work has been around about 160 years. Its historical roots are found within the Industrial Revolution of the early 1900s. It's a part of management DNA that has been very difficult to dislodge. Some say its way past its prime, but some form of it exists in many industries today, as most organizations are structured around the concept of command and control, or some variation of it.

Most likely, organizational structure resembles the following illustration.

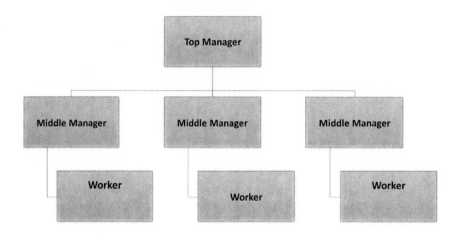

Some Thoughts on This Sort of Structure

1. It works great in the military structure of things. After all, command decisions involving life, death, attack, or retreat must be made by someone at the top.
2. Command and control runs contrary to how systems should be set up, implemented, and maintained.
3. Command and control resembles the differences between managing an enterprise and leading an enterprise.
4. Command and control stifles innovation and team orientation.
5. Command and control creates fear.

So why do so many organizations still utilize this approach? Once again, it's in our DNA. The following chart illustrates how command and control runs contrary to a modern systems way of thinking. Information may not be all-inclusive but provides a basis for the extreme differences.

Command and Control Thinking	Embodiment	Systems Approach and Thinking
Top down	**Viewpoint**	Part of a larger system
procedure driven	**how work is parceled**	value added
customer out	**customer orientation**	customer in
segregated	**decisions**	integrated
targets/outputs/ standards in relation to budgetary activity	**metrics**	variability, capability that is related to purpose of the organization
contractor driven	**supplier perspective**	cooperative/inclusive
management of people and budgets	**belief system**	how the processes are integrated
extrinsic value	**motivation drivers**	intrinsic value

As our workforce changes, the control exerted by those at the top face critical challenges. Command and control worked fine with the traditionalist generation, all of whom were impacted by the Great Depression of 1929 and who either fought or supported efforts during WWII. This was an accepted norm for them.

However, generations subsequent to this one have challenged the efficacy of such structures. Social norms of today and tomorrow will naturally resist attempts of workplace control. With technological advancements and improvements, workers will not necessarily be required to be at their workstations at a certain time, with heads down and producing. Newer technologies will require more emphasis on results-oriented outcomes rather than face-time control.

However, and as stated, the command and control structure has been difficult to abandon. Could this be part of the reason for low employee engagement numbers? For thirteen years, they have not changed, with the United States managing to engage around 30 percent of all workers, missing out on 70 percent of the remainder who have either checked out mentally or simply sit on the fence awaiting change.

Either way, inactivity of this magnitude costs the US economy trillions each year.

❺ Policies, procedures, and practices.

Most policies in organizations are written not for the majority but for the minority of employees who we call the "fringe 6 percent." These are the ones who reside outside the system norms. Old policies that don't address the needs of the modern workforce become just another management ritual.

This way of handling policies relates to the command and control system of managing people, outcomes, and budgets. Following are examples of real policies we have come across in our own journey of understanding profound leadership. There are many more examples we could have used, but these typify some very old, very arcane thinking and support our view of what constitutes very dismal practices.

> It is the policy of the company to restrict the use of toilet tissue to the rest areas.

Any employee found with toilet tissue outside the rest area will be subject to disciplinary action, up to and including termination of employment for repeated violations.

****

In order to promote excellent attendance, the company will incentivize employees to be at work on time and regularly. Each quarter, employees who achieve perfect attendance will receive three hundred dollars. To qualify for this reward, eligible employees must

Not miss any time from work, including:

(1) Vacation time
(2) Partial days such as doctor appointments
(3) Jury duty

****

To ensure consistent staffing of operations for individual locations, it is the policy of the company to limit the need for special absences.

Accordingly, should any employee require a special absence to attend weddings or funerals (not including those covered by death in the immediate family) will necessitate the employee to take the full week off. There will be no shift swapping allowed.

It must be noted these policies exist today. Not surprisingly, these organizations yield very high turnover, poor morale, and nonexistent employee engagement.

And people complain too, as demonstrated by a very real blog dedicated to poking fun at organizations and management. Here is a sampling of some of the ridicule directed at those ritualistic organizations.

- "I worked in a grocery store that had a little chart with everyone's name on it and they would put a gold star on there for a perfect register drawer. This is also how my parents' potty-trained my twin sister and me. They called it the hit-or-miss chart. And my eight-year-old brother came up with the idea. I could never take that seriously."
- "My old workplace decided to have a weekly compulsory company meeting that started (and finished) outside business hours."
- "I'm the only person in my office that isn't allowed to have my phone on or eat at my desk. I was banned after my boss said my food smelled too much, all the while ignoring the person across the office eating smoked mackerel."

Other practices create barriers as well.

All one has to do is look at the typical organization and the "probationary period." At a time of shrinking skill sets, demographic transitions, and other issues, organizations continue to use a defined period of time to evaluate newly hired employees. We believe this particular ritual has been handed down to us from the union era. This was a period of time employees would work for a company before being protected under the union contract. During this initial period, employees could be fired without retribution or grievance proceedings. This may be the reason for the beginning of the probationary period but does not explain why it must continue to exist today.

There are other mechanisms still in play at many companies including the temp-to-hire scenario. A person must undergo a gauntlet of sorts before being deemed worthy of the fraternity. Further practices such as these have a tendency to send the wrong message by instilling a lack of trust and lack of commitment early on. How are we able to extract commitment from employees when we fail to reciprocate?

These seemingly innocent practices send a signal of disengagement from the very beginning.

So is it any wonder employee engagement numbers are at a standstill? Once again, engagement cannot take hold as long as aged policies, procedures, and practices are kept in place. If organizations are ever going to get buy-in from employees, we simply must assure our practices match what we strive for.

❻ Internal competition is good!

Corporate America seems to think that internal competition is analogous to sports, where competition, winners, losers, and standings are established. As the late, great Ed Deming said, "This is wrong!"

As organizations move deeper into the future, competition for scarce resources and their recognition will become more intense. Many companies that foster internal competition among departments, divisions, and people will spend unproductive time competing with each other rather than working together. This is waste and creates a focus on people promoting their own agenda. When this is allowed to exist, the organization misses out on an opportunity to satisfy an organizational need. This in turn creates barriers that extend beyond the internal boundaries of the organization and may ultimately affect the end customer. It also goes against the grain in terms of systems thinking.

Yet for still unexplained reasons, many organizations find this healthy when research clearly indicates this is harmful. Returning to the performance-appraisal scenario, organizations which oftentimes generate stacked rankings, meaning pitching people against people, create undue and unnecessary internal strife. This of course affects teamwork, which is a myth that follows this one.

Companies argue that it helps separate the wheat from the chaff, especially in times of organization downsizing, which helps managers segregate the A players from the B players and B players from the C players. Our question is simple. Why hire C players in the first place? And if you don't hire them, what are you doing to make them C players?

In November 2013, the concept of forced (stacked) ranking was a top story in *Forbes Magazine* and the actions the new CEO had taken to rid the organization of the proverbial "dead wood." Once again, how did it get that way? Where was leadership? It didn't work for Microsoft, and it's doubtful it will work anywhere it's implemented. A competitive internal environment is not what organizations need or should desire in the end.

From an innovative perspective (and lots of innovation is needed in today's world), teams should be the focus, not the individual. In addition, identification and strengthening of competencies should take center stage. These simultaneously help the employee grow while the organization benefits. There is no doubt that competencies along with collaboration create better services and better products. However, there is a misguided notion in some companies that competition is healthy.

We know of a moderate-sized organization with multiple locations that promoted competition among the business units. They paid a moderate salary to the local operations managers but heavily rewarded them on the back end with huge performance bonuses and then set up competition among the branches. This competition created large windfalls for the individuals but did nothing to promote cooperation among units. Accordingly, each unit literally absconded work from each other, including underbidding projects to get the work and create volume. This created intense competitive behavior that made the workplace stressful and a lot less enjoyable.

The message that employees get from management might be purely in the reward system. When others see the individual who exhibits unhealthy, competitive, and aggressive behavior being rewarded, something becomes very clear. "That is what I have to do to get ahead." This undermines any sense of teamwork and collaboration. These two states cannot coexist and have interrelationship. If this is done, a mixed message is being transmitted throughout the organization.

Of course, internal competition creates infighting, as illustrated above. This oftentimes creates an us versus them quotient, both internally and externally, and many times affects community standing and a gridiron mentality.

Leadership has to be ultra-careful in regard to this; otherwise, it becomes a *Lord of the Flies* scenario. Teamwork would thus become an unobtainable goal. This brings us to our next myth and ritual: teamwork.

❼ We are a team!

Imagine the following scene.

> The location manager returns to work after attending a short workshop on organization and culture. He has a strong desire to improve teamwork. He announces that beginning immediately and going forward, teamwork is going to be the mantra, the new Grail. He feels productivity will soar, people will be happier, and the constant infighting will grind to a halt. He also feels customer service will improve, along with quality and corresponding financial metrics. He has high expectations of success!

> Six months later, there is no improvement in customer service, quality, or the financial picture. Teamwork has failed because people just didn't *get it.*

Scenes like this play out all across the United States. In this case, the location manager learned that teamwork is more than a pronouncement of ideas. He discovered too late that like all else in the modern sense, teamwork is based on a system of interrelated things. A false start has occurred.

Teams are not teams without a plan. People who are not accustomed to working together can't simply be put in a group without some skill building and understanding of teams and team behaviors.

So the myth is people can naturally work together without structure. But structure is exactly what teams need. Teams require many things to be effective. There are roles, responsibilities, behaviors, charters, and many other factors that must be considered. Of course, like many other "teams" before, they went into the process charged and ready to go. What they didn't have was a method to get there.

Brian Joiner, in his landmark book *The Team Handbook,* provides a succinct definition of a team: *a group of people pooling their skills, talents, and knowledge.* From this basis, we will tackle some nuances associated with teams. Once again, a team is not a team just because someone says it is. In fact, getting people to work toward a common goal requires a bit of work, understanding of tools, and an understanding of human behavior.

So what makes some teams highly effective while others languish and never accomplish much of anything? Let's examine some realities and characteristics within high functioning teams.

Ideal Teams

Attribute	Dynamic
Goals	The team members share a sense of purpose and common goals and each team member is willing to work to achieve these goals.
Process	The team is aware of and interested in its own processes and examines norms operating within the team.
Freedom of expression	Differences of opinion are encouraged and freely expressed. The team does not demand narrow conformity or adherence to formats that inhibit freedom of movement and expression.

Conflict and problem solving	The team is willing to identify conflict and focus on it until it is resolved or managed in a way that does not reduce the effectiveness of those involved. The team focuses on problem solving rather than allowing either interpersonal issues or competitive struggles to drain the team's energy.
Communications	The team members continually listen to and clarify what is being said and show interest in others thoughts and feelings.
Roles/sharing	Roles are balanced and shared to facilitate both the accomplishment of tasks and feelings of team cohesion and morale.
Resource allocation	The team identifies its own resources and uses them, depending on its needs. The team willingly accepts the influence and leadership of the members whose resources are relevant to the immediate need.
Creativity	To encourage risk taking and creativity, mistakes are treated as sources of learning rather than reasons for punishment.
Adaptability	The team is responsive to the changing needs of its members and to the external environment to which it is related.
Evaluation	Team members are committed to periodically evaluate the team's performance.
Growth	The members identify with the team and consider it a source of both professional and personal growth.
Trust	Developing a climate of trust is recognized as the crucial element for facilitating all the preceding characteristics.

However, there are some dangers associated with teams, especially ones which don't adhere to the previous illustrated team dynamics. Let's examine those found within a poor functioning team.

Dysfunctional Teams

Attribute	Dynamic
Harmony	Teams in which there is no conflict are not working the way they should. This does not mean there are personal attacks taking place, but if one team member does not feel they can challenge another member (including the team leader), the danger of groupthink and/or subversion of the process is magnified.
One leader	Teams which do not share leadership are missing out on the majority of team talents. This is not to say that a single person may not be designated as the team leader for a certain project but that during a project every team member must be able (and willing) to step into the leader role.
Distractions	If all views are not surfaced during team meetings, you can bet that the opposing views will emerge in myriad ways later. If you are seeing (or taking part in) side conversation, be aware that there is a problem.
Suppression	If during a conversation with another team member you find yourself saying, "What a great idea. Why didn't you bring that up during the meeting?" that's a sure sign of trouble. Members should be enabled to express themselves freely.
Cliques	It is natural for one team member to be more drawn to one member than to another. However, if tight cliques have formed and during tough discussions sides are taken quickly along party lines, the team is not working at its potential.

Forming a team takes a bit of deliberation in order to avoid "Let's throw something together to resolve (whatever)."

As mentioned earlier, teams are developed and it takes time to evolve into a harmonious group. To this end, leadership has to understand the critical areas of team development. It must be noted that many teams never achieve their desired results based on previously illustrated barriers.

Most teams follow a prescribed path from beginning to end, as illustrated in the following sequence.

1. Forming
2. Storming
3. Norming
4. Performing
5. Assessment and disbandment

In the *forming* stage of team development, team members don't know each other well enough to trust each other. This is the polite and get-acquainted state of team development. After this phase, when team members get to know and trust each other, confrontations, conflicts, and frustrations are allowed to surface. Once teams accept the fact that *storming* is common and civil disagreements are encouraged, they pass to the next stage of development. This is the *norming* stage, where they develop operating rules and procedures in order to function smoothly. In the *performing* state, team members know each other and have resolved any personal or task conflicts and are applying their energy to whatever task they are facing. It must be noted, though, that most teams have difficulty achieving this high level of performance.

A good analogy of high performance is a basketball player. For most of the game, he or she runs up and down the floor, setting plays and attempting to score with jump shots, hook shots, etc. However, in the rare times the ball is dunked, the basketball player reaches a pinnacle level of performance, where he or she leaves the basketball floor for a few seconds to soar above the rim for the dunk. This is usually followed by *oohs* and *ahs* of the fans and even the courtside announcers. High-level performance is achieved! However, this high level of performance is difficult to repeat time and again.

In the *assessment and disbandment* stage, the team reviews what they were tasked to do and then disband with a fresh sense of what was and what was not accomplished. This is the reflective stage of team development where true learning occurs.

So how is leadership disbursed and how are decisions made in a team environment? The following illustration helps in understanding the dynamics associated with leader-centered and team-centered "leadership." It illustrates power and authority and the differences between a leader-centered team and a team-centered one.

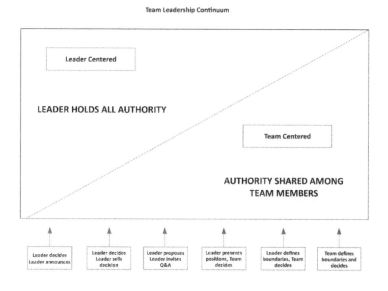

When a team develops along this continuum, more and more members are able to experience being a leader, as well as serving as a member. One thing to keep in mind is that, depending on the situation, the placement of where the team finds itself on the continuum may vary with each experience.

Natural Work Team (NWT) versus Project Team

There are basically two types of teams which leaders will have involvement with on a consistent basis. One is the natural work team and the other is the project team. The two are different based on the following characteristics:

Natural Work Team (NWT)	Project Team
exists in all organizational structures	exists for the duration of a project and then disbands
a supervisor and his or her subordinates make up a NWT	are not permanent to the organization
are permanent to the organization	works on issues narrow in scope but likely to improve things
represent a team focus to managing the organization	has an optimal operating level of 7 members +/- 2 (no less than 5 and no more than 9)
usually owns a process	is chartered by the NWT or other leadership groups
may "charter" a project team to improve deficiencies	is time bound, with a definite beginning and end

Initiating a Project Team

When starting a team to work on a specific project, the following things must be considered.

First, among the numerous items that make a team truly high performing are the right size, support, and decision-making authority.

So what is the correct size of a team? Usually, this depends on several factors, but the team must be large enough to cross-pollinate ideas and small enough to be able to work together. The rule of thumb of an optimum-performing team usually centers around seven members, +/-2. This creates the best effectiveness. Too large a workgroup becomes a mob or a committee to nowhere, and too small ideas are limited and collaboration is jeopardized.

A team also needs a clear direction and support. This means members know their roles both in the organization and on the team. They must also be aware of the boundaries by which the team functions. Leadership understands the nature and function of the team and has expectations the team will produce results.

Also, teams do not normally vote. Their goal is to arrive by consensus. However, consensus takes longer but does not produce zero-sum game, which roughly translates into "I win; you lose." Voting and democratic tenets have a tendency to create this win/lose barrier and are usually avoided. Consensus allows a team member to support the team's decision while not necessarily agreeing with the final decision. Notwithstanding this, there are some areas where a form of voting is used, such as multi-voting. Remember that consensus is not total agreement. Consensus simply means "I may disagree but I will support the decision of the team." Agreeing to disagree is an option and not a barrier to outcomes.

In addition, teams have task differentiation. Members recognize those situations where it is appropriate to work independently, in pairs, or as a team.

Teams have shared leadership. In various team situations, the leadership role may shift to whoever has the expertise, without the appointed leader feeling threatened or his or her influence lessened. Shared leadership involves assuring peak performance under any and all circumstances.

One of the most critical elements of team development, along with team success, hinges on knowing what to work on, how to solve problems, and what limits are placed on the team. In project teams, it is absolutely essential to have these parameters established.

Chartering: The Key to Success

A fundamental way to assure the correct start, execution, and completion of a project is utilizing a team charter. A team charter has the following components:

1. It clarifies team roles and responsibilities, such as facilitator, note taker, and team leader.
2. A charter clearly defines what the team will work on and requires the proper descriptor of the team's function. This is a statement at the beginning that must be clear, succinct, and within the overall parameters of what needs to be solved. Too broad of charter statement will cause the team to wander off in various directions, and a too narrow one will limit the team's ability to effectively diagnose the issue.

3. A charter establishes and determines ground rules for team management, such as agendas, process checks, follow-up, and follow-through.
4. Determination of what team training the team requires. As mentioned earlier, a team is not a team just because someone calls it a team. The training may include team-building exercises, use of tools and methods, and problem-solving processes.

❽ Happiness creates engagement.

Happiness is a state of mind that can go up and down at any point in time. Happiness therefore does not create engagement, but active disengagement affects an organization's bottom line.

As stated earlier, employee engagement is a very hot topic in the United States today, as it should be. When so many employees are disengaged, a level of discomfort and unease exists, especially for leadership. The percentage of employees who are *actively* disengaged (roughly 18 percent) cost US employers upward of $550 billion dollars each year. Over the course of time, since the first engagement study was released, this adds up to trillions of dollars in lost productivity and earnings for organizations. Even though seemingly elusive, this concept is absolutely worth pursuing.

Part of this is due to real numbers. Organizations with an average of 9.3 *engaged* employees for every actively disengaged employee in 2010–2011 experienced 147 percent higher earnings per share compared to their competition. Those with an average of 2.6 engaged employees for every actively disengaged employee experienced 2 percent lower earnings per share when compared to the competition during that same time period.

For illustration purposes, the following chart is a historical representation of employee engagement from the first release of the Gallup survey in 2000 through 2012.

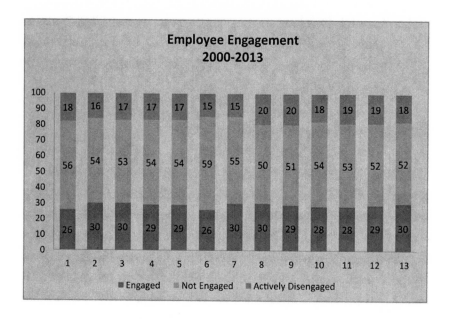

Essentially, employee engagement has flat-lined with virtually no movement up or down in thirteen years. This is in spite of good and bad economic times and different workforces.

So doesn't it make sense to work on increasing employee engagement and satisfaction? We think so.

Furthermore, it may be worth thinking about this in terms of employee happiness. For example, happy employees are less likely to feel excess stress at work. Their overall mood is more upbeat. According to research conducted by the *Wall Street Journal,* happier workers help their colleagues 33 percent more often than unhappy employees. Happy employees also achieve their goals 31 percent more often and are 36 percent more intrinsically motivated in their work.

While happiness does not ensure employee engagement, happy employees generate a cycle of positive reinforcement that helps sustain their level of engagement and satisfaction even when things get tough. On the other hand, an actively disengaged employee may be happy about a single benefit or perk yet still fail to *contribute* at the level of an engaged employee. Furthermore, striving to keep employees happy by simply indulging them will not necessarily increase employee engagement.

We should focus first on employee engagement and satisfaction. Employee happiness will follow. But is the reverse the case? Perks without purpose may provide a short-term happiness boost, but most employees are more internally motivated by meaning and a sense of connection.

Here are a few things you can do to foster engagement in your workplace:

Provide Meaning and Alignment

Workers crave meaning. They want to feel like they are part of something bigger than themselves—and to understand how they contribute value to the organization. Some need to feel aligned with the company's stance on the environment or social responsibility. Others are content to be valued team members who understand and support the company vision and mission.

Offer Opportunities for Growth, Education, and Advancement

In a study completed in 2012, The Society of Human Resources Management (SHRM) found that jobseekers in the US rank growth and professional development as their top priority. More recently, in its annual study, Career Bliss identified the "50 Happiest Companies in America" and revealed much about what contributes to employee happiness and engagement. Across the thousands of employee reviews analyzed, there were two factors that younger employees in particular identified most often as key determinants of their satisfaction and happiness at work: challenge and opportunities for learning and growth. This is especially important since keeping today's young professionals (the most mobile workers since Tinkers traveled!) engaged is a common HR preoccupation these days.

Make Recognition Part of Your Culture

Recognition benefits both the giver and the receiver. There is an extensive body of research supporting the value of specific, valid recognition and employee satisfaction. What is less documented is the impact that recognition has on the giver. A growing body of research, much of it produced by Adam Grant, a professor at Wharton School, shows that employees who give recognition and reward gain as much benefit as the person being recognized or rewarded. Science supports his belief with mounting evidence that expressing gratitude and recognizing others is good for our health, productivity, and happiness.

Build Trust

One of the single biggest contributors to employee happiness is a culture of trust: feeling trusted and being able to trust the people we work with and the organizations we work for. One Harvard University study showed that trust was a key factor in creating successful, productive workplaces. Nancy Etcoff, PhD, lead researcher on the study, concluded, "Workplaces that provide positive environments that foster interpersonal trust and quality personal relationships create the most committed and productive employees."

Strive for open communication, respect, honesty, transparency, follow-through, and real accountability to help build trust in your organization.

Be Flexible

Flexibility is one of the factors that rank high on both employee happiness (Career Bliss, Georgetown University) and employee engagement (Gallup). The employer, who embraces flexible work hours, locations, and policies that all help reduce employee stress and support work-life balance, will reap the benefits of happier, more engaged workers.

All these will be explored more thoroughly throughout the remainder of this book.

Chapter 3

Systems: An Effective Leadership Path

All of the empowered, motivated, teamed-up, self-directed, incentivized, accountable, reengineered, and reinvented people you can muster cannot compensate for a dysfunctional system. When the system is functioning well, these other things are all just foofaraw[1]. When the system is not functioning well, these things are still only empty, meaningless twaddle.[2]
—Peter R. Scholtes

Peter R. Scholtes nailed it. Systems, established and understood, can and will move an organization to the results they are looking for. Slogans, fads, and other trivial pursuits will not.

The individual who is not well versed in system thinking may only view a system in the technological sense. However, there is a much more universal view to be had. A system includes not only technology but a human equation as well.

Systems are a set of interactions and interdependencies on a large scale. They have purpose, they have processes interrelated with each other, and they represent how things are done and how things are accomplished. They also have the following characteristics.

- Systems have structure by components, elements, and their composition.

---

[1] *Foofaraw* means a great fuss over something trivial.
[2] *Twaddle* means nonsensical. See the definition of *baloney*.

- Systems have behaviors, which involves inputs, processing and outputs of material, energy, information, or data.
- Systems have interconnectivity: the various parts of a system have functional as well as structural relationships to each other.
- Systems may have some functions or groups of functions such as processes.
- Systems have boundaries. This helps prevent poorly constructed decisions regarding change to the system by eliminating interference with another system.

Two ways to look at systems can be found in the example of the automobile and the human body. Both are systems in the classic sense.

Let's look at the automobile first.

The purpose of an automobile is generally to provide meaningful transportation (unless you are cruising the beach in a tricked-out convertible). In order to do this economically, efficiently, and safely, a bunch of different operating processes must come together. It needs tires, steering, propulsion, lights, horn, transmission, etc. The key thing to remember about a system is this: the process operating alone cannot deliver the intended result. The processes support the system but cannot alone take care of the need.

To clarify further, let's break it down using the vehicle example. The major support systems of an automobile are power train, fuel, steering, and electrical. The vehicle is not able to operate safely and efficiently without these major supporting processes and systems (recognizing the vehicle itself is the system of transportation).

Now let's look at one process, that being steering. For steering to work properly, it requires tires and wheels and a steering column. These items by themselves cannot power the automobile, and the automobile must have other processes working in support to provide transportation. All processes, therefore, must work in unison to achieve the need.

The human body acts in much the same manner. You have a circulatory system, adrenal system, digestive system, musculoskeletal system, and so on. The body is dependent on this for a total system; neither of them can operate outside the system and none of them are stand-alone. They must act in concert with each other, and when they don't, there is a breakdown of the system that causes sickness, debilitation, and even death.

It is the same way in any organization. The healthier the supporting processes, the healthier the system. A breakdown of the processes creates problems within the entire system.

So let's explore this concept even further.

What Is a Process?

In simple terms, process refers to the individual components of a system. Just as a system has purpose, so does process, except in isolation, the process is incapable of achieving the purpose of a system.

Processes are then supported by methods. These are the fundamental parts of the process and again have their own purpose. However, the value attributed to the method can be seen only through the interactions it has with other methods supporting the process. Methods, in turn, are supported by steps and may be considered an invaluable piece of it. Steps interact with other steps to serve the purpose of the method.

A total system view is shown below using Honda Motor Company as an example.

Worldwide Honda Motor Co. Ltd.	
large view	Honda automobiles, motorcycles, power equipment, engines, robots, aircraft, solar cells, mountain bikes
microcosm view	a Honda product line
process	selling a Honda car
method	showing a customer how to use the navigation tool in the car

Of course, the commonality among systems and process and methods is the actual chain of events which produce something of value, be it a widget or a service. This involves understanding suppliers, inputs, process, output, and customers.

Dr. Ed. Deming perfected this systematic way of looking at how all work is performed in every organization, whether or not it's understood that all work is a process. To fulfill the need(s) of the customer, both internal and external, requires an understanding of the purpose (end use) of what is being produced.

Dr. Deming liked to use the example of a "clean" table. Without understanding the purpose, it would be impossible to clean. He elaborated on this by explaining cleaning a table used for eating food is quite different from cleaning a table where surgical operations are performed. To ask someone to clean the table without understanding purpose creates an impossible situation and, of course, great confusion. Understanding systems and process and methods helps people clearly understand expectations. Without a clear understanding, we leave too much to the imagination and inadvertently set in motion unknown delivery expectations, which leads to disappointment and failure.

Old Paradigms and SIPOC

Unfortunately, many organizations are still mired in the old paradigm of command and control structure of organizations, as introduced in chapter 2. Many continue to rely on the organizational chart to understand how things happen. This sort of mind-set has been difficult to overcome.

To fully appreciate systems and processes, we need to think differently about the organizational structure. In today's world, the rapid speed of change, global competition, and other factors create a need for a more agile organization that responds quicker to customers. This starts with understanding suppliers, inputs, process, outcomes, and customers, or SIPOC for short.

Whenever we look at a traditional organizational chart, we are tempted to see our direct supervision and those in higher positions as the "customer." However, SIPOC is how work is accomplished.

Dr. Deming was the first to recognize the organization as a system and developed his view of it. This is simulated below.

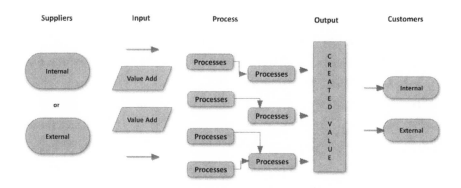

SIPOC model

This SIPOC model enables people to visually determine how things are done, which is in sharp contrast to the traditional view of organizations. SIPOC enunciates purpose whereas attempting to find purpose in a traditional organizational view is extremely difficult, if not impossible. Understanding the purpose for any activity helps provide that extra layer of clarity that may be missing. When expectations are surpassed, there are pleasing outcomes. However, when expectations fall below, the desired result is normally disappointment.

Purpose

> Efforts and courage are not enough
> without purpose and direction.
> —John F. Kennedy

Without purpose and direction, we have no idea where to go. Purpose helps us define what business or service we are in. More importantly though, it helps define what business we are not in!

Generally, customers relate to the purpose by the interactions with the organization. In other words, organizations whose sole purpose is to make money more than likely will not have customers. Why? There is not an altruistic or higher calling associated with just making money. In other words, they are not trying to satisfy a need of a customer; they just want money! As stated earlier, there are many illegal activities associated with simply making money that will preclude any organization from having customers, at least the kind who openly are able to boast of your products or services. For this reason, purpose is essential to a successful organization.

Purpose provides direction.

If carburetor manufactures would have seen a clearer and futuristic purpose associated with internal engine combustion, they would never have relinquished the business to manufacturers of fuel injectors. There are many other products and services that have failed to understand this, and they are no longer in business.

Accordingly, having purpose drives the business and provides a compass along the way. It helps the system perform at optimum levels. Without a purpose, the system is likely to become dysfunctional ... and expensive to operate!

A Systems View

So what does a system look like? To provide an idea of a system, the following is a view of a typical HR system and corresponding linkages found in most organizations. Linkage is a fundamental step in understanding how parts of an individual system fit together. In this example, HR has various pieces that are interconnected. This helps illustrate the importance of looking at the entire system whenever changes are made to it. Changing things without regard to how they affect things upstream or downstream causes people frustration, anxiety, and needless waste.

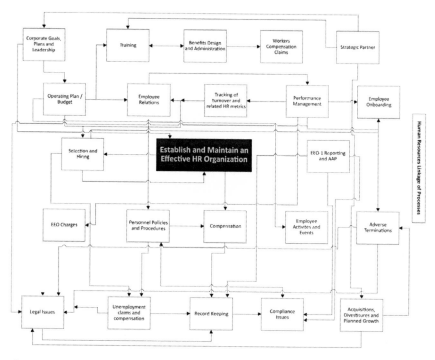

©Innova Management Consulting, 2003

Linkage of Processes

This illustration shows how all processes are linked and aligned within the HR system. Later on, we will visit some concepts of systems behavior, but for now, this linkage demonstrates the vital relationship with various processes found within a typical human resources department.

Another view of a system follows. This is a little easier to understand and less detailed. However, it clearly shows how all things come together to produce something of value.

Both illustrations have a "mainstay." What differs from the first linkage is how the processes are used for varying purposes within the system itself.

XYZ Motors

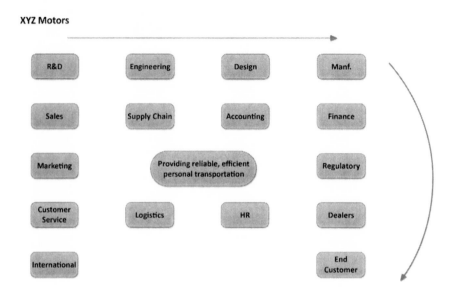

In this mythical car company XYZ Motors, the major functions (which are systems within a system) must work with each other to produce the mainstay of "reliable, efficient personal transportation." There are multiple interrelationships necessary to get the product to the customer, including external suppliers providing parts and even completed assemblies as well as other services.

Leadership drives the entire organization to achievement of its mission, but it also influences all parts of the system, whether logistics, manufacturing, R&D, and so forth.

In short, leadership is fundamentally important for overall success of the entire system.

Systemic Thinking

The heart of profound leadership requires fundamental knowledge of systems and its relation to systemic thinking. By looking at things holistically, one can arrive at better solutions, in less time and *with less cost.*

Peter Senge extensively explored systems thinking in *The Fifth Discipline* as it pertained to learning in organizations. Senge's work was issued in the latter part of the twentieth century, but today his work and analysis are just as relevant and revealing as they were over thirty years ago. Understanding what systems do and don't do becomes necessary when thinking in this regard.

Following are key learning points which were first expressed by Peter Senge. These are of paramount importance and make sense when reinforcing the need for systems thinking now and well beyond.

Too Narrow of a Focus

As leaders, we have a tendency to be puzzled by causes of problems and rely on our experiences in solving issues to other seemingly related problems. This affects our focus and sometimes narrows it. Our reactions to the problem may not necessarily resolve the new issue, even though apparently related.

How many times do leaders respond to a stimulus by utilizing these experiences? Focusing on only one process rather than viewing the entire system for the optimum solution may create a random, disconnected emphasis resulting in blaming rather than problem resolution. By narrowing your focus, you will be drawn to looking for a culprit rather than the system that produced the result.

Solutions which shift problems are not solutions at all. However, a systemic way of viewing the whole lessens the reliance on this and reduces the chance that your "solution" becomes someone else's "problem."

Solutions Require Holistic Thought

In systems thinking, there is a thing Senge called "compensating feedback." This occurs when interventions create solutions that have adverse consequences. This is essentially tampering with the system to create a solution.

For instance, to combat greenhouse gases, the federal government required a new blend of 10 percent ethanol be added to gasoline in those areas where smog was outside the normal ranges. Ethanol is derived from corn. Farmers were happy and began planting an abundance of corn crops since the mandates allowed corn to be less of a commodity type of crop.

However, the feds now allowed the food supply to be used as a source of fuel. Corn crops meant for the food supply now were being used for the fuel supply. There were spikes in all corn prices, which affected the total cost of food. Anything made from corn went through price spirals. To get an idea of how corn is used in food products, all one simply has to do is look randomly at everyday products found in home pantries to see this idea was a bad one.

The United States food supply should have never been used as an energy source.

There are many other examples of this on both a personal and larger system point of view.

Rash Decisions Create Consequences

What this means is that without looking at issues systemically, quick solutions to an issue rarely resolve it permanently. Short-term fixes feel good, but without eliminating the problem in its entirety, they may resurface down the road. Leaders are notorious for "fixing" things based on the way they have been taught, but fixing things only for a short term and lessening pain points will exacerbate the problem later.

The most notable example of this may be the way the federal government looks at fixing social problems. Another may be the way organizations respond to customer complaints. Offering them a discount coupon may soften the customer in the short term but does nothing to eliminate the problem in the long term.

There is a story from many years ago that illustrates this well.

> A certain political figure became embroiled in a public controversy. Eventually, he was asked to resign. His replacement was named, and as the new appointee was settling in his new office, he opened the top desk drawer and found three envelopes, labeled 1, 2, and 3.
>
> Envelope 1 had additional written instructions, which said, "Open whenever controversy arises." Sure enough, a controversy arose and the press began hounding him. It became uncomfortable so he opened envelope 1. Written inside was "Blame it on your predecessor." He did, and the controversy died down.

However, additional things were discovered and he was once again embroiled in the same controversy. As things heated up, he opened envelope 2, which read, "Deny it." He did, and once again things died down a bit. However, not for long. In the next few days, the media began its assault again. Desperate, the politician opened the third and final envelope.

Envelope 3 read, "Make three envelopes."

The point of the story is this: nothing is solved by taking the easy route. Only through understanding and applying systemic solutions will issues be permanently resolved.

Uncovering the Real Problem

Senge illustrates a great story to highlight the point of uncovering the real problem.

A passerby encounters a drunk on his hands and knees under a street lamp. He offers to help and learns the drunk is looking for his house keys. After some time spent searching in vain, he asks where the drunk dropped them. The drunk indicates that he had dropped them outside his front door. The passerby then asks why he was looking for the keys so far away from the front door, whereupon the drunk tells him, "There is no lighting by the front door."

The real learning is this: easy solutions are not necessarily the *best* solutions. Of course, looking for ones keys would be easier in light, if the key was indeed lost there. In this story, the real cause of the problem was there was no lighting at the front door, yet this fact was completely overlooked due to concentration on one part of the problem: a lost key.

In other words, when we work on a part of the system without understanding the system in totality, we may be working on the wrong thing at the wrong time and in the wrong way.

Fostering an Epidemic

We can look at the current structure of the federal government, especially in light of the past few years using government stimulus to grow the economy. Key learning appears here as short-term interventions and has seemingly fed into long-term addictions.

From 2008 to mid-2012, the federal government, under two separate and distinct administrations, spent a trillion dollars on stimulus to kick-start the US economy.

The stimulus was used to prop up the financial industry and the automobile industry, but also money was given to states to help keep teachers, firefighters, and police on the job. In addition, there were hopes that shovel-ready jobs would employ displaced workers. Finally, as part of the massive government interventions, unemployment benefits were extended to ninety-nine weeks, which is almost two years. Following are the effects of such efforts.

- Money loaned to financial institutions to prop them up may never be fully paid back, with billions of dollars still outstanding.
- States used the stimulus money to help balance state budgets and not create jobs for the economy.

- Shovel-ready jobs were not readily available. The ones that were created averaged around $200,000 per job. There is still need for massive rebuilding of infrastructure in the United States, but the funds were spent elsewhere.
- Studies have shown that ninety-nine weeks of extended unemployment benefits did not necessarily help. People would wait until nearly the end of the lapse of benefits before they seriously began looking for a job.

In Senge's view of the cure for this problem, which wasn't even thought about at the time of his writing *The Fifth Discipline*, interventions of this sort create an epidemic rather than a solution to the problem.

The system is fundamentally weakened by virtue of looking at things independently rather than viewing as a whole.

Putting the Cart before the Horse Is Doing Things in the Wrong Order

One of the fundamental flaws in past management thinking is based on faster is better. More products out the door increase profit! We must grow! Growth is good!

Are these things fundamentally accurate? Let's examine some pertinent issues of this through another story.

> The principals saw an opportunity to grow their small company into one that could be a major player in a particular market. Borrowing on the worth of the present company, the principals bought a smaller company. They decided to be more aggressive and go with an initial public offering to raise cash.

The idea was to be a major holding company and simply let the acquired organizations grow organically enough to purchase similar types of smaller operations. With their aggressive plan for growth, their stock soared and reached a milestone of being the second fastest growing stock on the NASDAQ exchange. With this newfound fame and bravado, they decided to capitalize further and began announcing deals before they were consummated.

They continued on their aggressive acquisitions, now offering the high stock price in exchange for ownership. This continued until one of their announced acquisitions pulled out of the for-sale market.

In the meantime, their acquisitions did not yield the growth they anticipated so they began to make "management changes" to the leadership of the acquired organizations, not realizing that the old leadership was the horsepower behind the acquired organizations' steadfastness. They instituted new controls and added people to run the organizations who did not have the skill set, clear idea, purpose, vision, or depth of knowledge of the people they replaced.

Wall Street did not like what it perceived as broken promises. The stock began to fall, just a little at first but enough to make investors nervous. The stock failed to show any signs of rebound, and no amount of press releases could stop the next sequence of events.

The stock went into a free fall and within eighteen months, the darlings of Wall Street had become pariahs.

The stock became worthless, and even one of the acquired companies, with a highly reputable name in their respective market, was declared bankrupt by the principals to make way for an asset sale.

In the span of two years, a once promising organization became essentially worthless. This company no longer exists in *any form.*

What is the lesson here? In the story above, a few lessons are worth mentioning.

- First, leadership was simply not capable of making the right call. Their strength was in running organizations on a much smaller scale, such as is found in command and control type organizations.
- Second, their inflated stock price, not to mention their inflated self-worth, spelled disaster.
- Third, people were hired to replace experienced and senior leadership. Purpose was clouded and a failure to understand competencies of the departing personnel went unrecognized. They simply hired the wrong people with insufficient skill sets to make the acquisitions work. The result is the acquisitions failed.
- Fourth, they tried to grow too fast without having first obtained sufficient operating efficiencies necessary for growth.
- Finally, they simply were proven to be incompetent in the end. They took a few successes and attempted to recreate them on a larger scale. The final price? Around 2,500 good people lost their jobs and a good number of the internal employees and stockholders lost their investment.

Too much growth without a plan to assure success—unfortunately, this same scenario is repeated many times each year. Systems can be complex at times. As Senge aptly noted, "A little knowledge is a dangerous thing."

Haste Makes Waste

Effects are the symptoms of problems while *causes* are really the items that create the effects. Too often, leaders think there are linear relationships between cause and effect. In the example of government intervention into the food supply being used as a fuel source, the effects experienced were not time related. It took several years, but even the proponents of using corn as a fuel source finally admitted this was not a good idea. In fact, in the United States, the entire population is paying a much higher price for food as a result of this decision, which was actually implemented three administrations ago.

Accordingly, this proves that haste makes waste. The need for speed and leadership's reliance on quick answers to complex problems cloud vision and shield the real view.

Haste indeed makes waste.

Getting the Biggest Bang for the Buck

Senge states that many people have called systems thinking the "dismal science" because it proves that the most obvious solutions simply don't work. Systems thinking points out obvious solutions improve matters in the short term and risk taking makes things much worse in the long term.

However, small and acutely focused actions many times produce much greater improvements. He calls this phenomenon "leverage." We know that having leverage means we have the upper hand or may be more effective than another. Thus, finding the place in a system to address them to have the most effect demands a study of all processes within a system in order to find the trigger point. There is no easy way to determine where you will reap the most benefits from and obtain the biggest bang for your buck. Your search may bring you to the least obvious of processes, but thoroughness and patience are keys to finding the solution that will stick long-term.

Assumptions Block Realities

Changing our paradigm of how we view things, especially from a system perspective, allows us greater vision. Many times, issues which appear to be real dilemmas are not necessarily so from a systems point of view.

As Senge noted many years ago, American manufacturing thought they had to choose between quality and speed of production. We were even taught in business school that quality control professionals had divergent goals with production professionals and while they could coexist, they could not agree. "Quality costs more" was the mantra of the day! Over time, this has been proven very wrong.

By revamping systems, understanding process behaviors, eliminating waste and rework, and building quality into products and services, it has been proven that quality produces things that do not cost more; they cost less. The total cost of quality, when measured properly, establishes a mechanism to produce high quality at a lower cost, something that was unthinkable thirty short years ago.

Today, core systems competencies of leaders should include the following:

- systems and interrelationships
- quality and variability
- speed to market
- customer service
- information and learning
- global
- change

Any leader of an organization who does not understand the need and utilization of these skills simply will fail in today's market conditions and organizational focus. These skills require *systems thinking* to be effective.

A Complete Puzzle Needs All the Pieces

Whenever leadership looks at only part of the system as a cause of dilemmas, problems, etc., they are more than likely to create an even greater issue, problem, or dilemma. Making a change within the system without looking at the consequences of that decision may help only the one area being scrutinized. In fact, performance can be improved beyond what was the original intent. However, looking only at one aspect of the problem, the resulting "solution" may cause deleterious effects on other parts.

This is why we need to look at the *entire system* to assure whatever changes are made do not have unintentional consequences elsewhere.

Senge illustrates this by suggesting how looking at just one part of a system leads to false conclusions. The poem "Blind Men and the Elephant" by John Godfrey Saxe helps drive this point home.

At various times, each of us has a tendency to look at parts of things rather than the complete picture. In systems, this can prove to be disastrous because of our failure to understand interrelationships of parts that make the whole. The fable provides insight into the relativity, cloudiness, or inexpressible nature of truth, the behavior of experts in fields where there is a deficit or inaccessibility of information, the need for communication, and respect for different perspectives.

The term for this is *diversity* as first introduced, which will be elaborated on in chapter 5.

Here is the fable though.

It was six men of Indostan
To learning much inclined,
Who went to see the Elephant
(Though all of them were blind),
That each by observation
Might satisfy his mind
The *First* approach'd the
Elephant,
And happening to fall
Against his broad and sturdy
side,
At once began to bawl:
"God bless me! but the
Elephant
is very like a wall"

The *Second*, feeling of the
tusk,
Cried, "Ho what have we here
So very round and smooth
and sharp?
To me 'tis mighty clear
This wonder of an Elephant
Is very like a spear!"
The *Third* approached the
Animal,
And happening to take
The squirming trunk within
Hid hands,
Thus boldly up and spake:
"I see," quoth he. "the
Elephant
Is very like a snake!"

The *Fourth* reached out his
eager hand,
And he felt about the knee,
"What most this wondrous
beast is like
Is mighty plain," quoth he,
Tis clear enough the
Elephant
Is very like a tree!"
The *Fifth* who chanced to
touch the ear,
Said: "E'en the blindest man
Can tell what this resembles
most;
Deny the fact who can,

This marvel of an Elephant
Is very like a fan!"
The *Sixth* no sooner had
Begun
about the beast to grope,
Then, seizing on the swinging tail
That fell within his
scope,
"I see," quoth he, "the
Elephant
Is very like a rope!"
And so these men of
Indostan
Disputed loud and long,
Each in his own opinion
Exceeding stiff and
strong,
Though each was partly
in the right, And all were
in the wrong!

In many organizations of yesteryear, as well as today, people are simply not allowed to have full access to important, vital information necessary for them to make "the right call." While not everything can be clearly seen from the larger view, a too narrow focus creates our individual perspectives, which doesn't lend itself to determining the truth.

In the fable above, each blind man "saw" something different based on where he stood in relation to others. This must be avoided in the business world. This is possible whenever the system is viewed systemically.

Rising and Falling as One

Dr. Ed Deming wrote his fourteen points philosophy to enable managers and leaders to begin thinking about a new way of conducting business. His point 8 stated, "Drive out fear so that everyone may work effectively for the company." Fear inside any organization creates finger-pointing, CYA, or whatever term best fits self-protection.

An excellent philosophy for leaders to adopt would be Deming's eighth point: *drive out fear.* Human nature creates a tendency for people to blame inside as well as outside forces for various problems. However, there should be no blame, just opportunities for solutions.

Fear causes people to blame.

Why Variation Is Important

To understand variation is to attain one of the four components of profound knowledge.

Profound knowledge as described by Dr. Deming encompasses understanding variation, the theory of management, psychology and learning and systems thinking. These items understood in conjunction with each other allow the new leader to lead the organization in whatever direction it needs to go, irrespective of outside influences, including disruptive technology.

However, leaders have been taught to focus mostly on tabular results, usually only after something has transpired, such as financial numbers and incidents. While there is nothing wrong with looking at results in this manner, making decisions based on "tabular" results exclusively may cause leaders to look at the wrong information, in the wrong way, and at the wrong time.

Understanding variation helps to look at the systems holistically rather than in a series of singular data points.

One example of variation is deviation that inherently resides in systems. The following scenario helps in understanding how to look at data. This scenario has occurred many times over the past several years and the outcome is always the same. Leadership arrives at the wrong answer each and every time!

Imagine a location manager getting a report one month that indicates his operation experienced eleven safety incidents in a month. He knows five are the average his operation experiences but eleven is unacceptable. His concern turns into an order to fix this. Sure enough, the next month, incidents are reduced to a normal level. However, less than six months, later the monthly report indicates ten incidents occurred. Once again the order goes out to fix the issue, and sure enough, the incidents drop to about the average per month. Problem solved!

Another eight months pass, and the location found itself once again experiencing eleven safety incidents. Apparently, it wasn't solved after all.

The truth is nothing will be solved until the system is changed. What the location manager is seeing is an example of not looking at things systemically. He and the location are reacting to a series of singular data points, making changes that are not changes at all. Perhaps they did more awareness, perhaps a bit more training, and even instilling some fear of reporting incidents.

It takes looking at things in a new and correct way to understand how effective change and improvement occur. Look at the following chart. Of course, there were a few months of increased incidents. Some months showed eleven while others experienced ten. But has anything changed? Has anything really improved?

Month	Incidents	Month	Incidents	Month	Incidents	Month	Incidents
January	6	July	4	January	2	July	10
February	3	August	8	February	6	August	3
March	2	September	10	March	4	September	0
April	4	October	6	April	7	October	5
May	11	November	3	May	11	November	7
June	7	December	6	June	4	December	0

It appears something positive happened as incidents decreased after each high month was recorded and acted upon. However, focusing on those solely in isolation and making changes to them created no real change.

So yes, things got better in June but went back up in September. They went down again the following month but were back up to eleven in May the following year. Once again, they decreased but by July were up yet again.

The only way to realistically view this sort of pattern is on a statistical process control chart. When viewed in this manner, one actually sees the real variation that transpired. This is noted in the following chart.

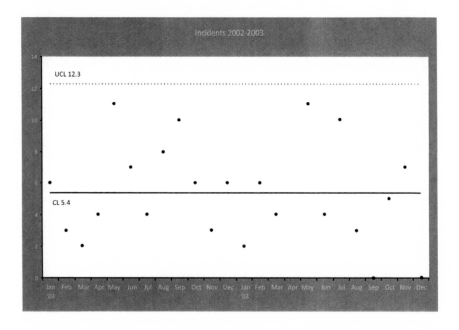

When trained to read it properly, one sees that only normal, random variation occurred over the two years. In fact, this variation will continue with some months experiencing the norms and other months experiencing perceived abnormal. This means in any given month the system will produce from zero to twelve incidents … until the system is changed.

Random variation will persist, no matter how much pleading or cajoling transpires. The system is delivering results for which it was designed. Without applying a consistent, established system, the results will continue to be randomly delivered. But with a system in place and utilizing systems thinking, the leader in empowered to look at things differently and with an eye toward improvement.

Understanding variation and its consequences helps the leader lead better. Period.

Chapter 4

Finding Purpose: Mission, Vision, and Values: The Foundation of Leadership

---

Your beliefs become your thoughts, your thoughts
become your words, your words become your actions,
your actions become your habits, your habits become
your values, and your values become your destiny.
—Gandhi

The blog post below encapsulates what many people feel about how an organization constructs mission, vision, and values and the sense of what is really accomplished with the final version. Jane Logan has the wisdom and the ability to capture key thoughts so eloquently.

> Mission, vision, and values are supposed to be the North Star of strategic planning, the beacon by which organizations set their strategic compasses and then align their everyday priority settings. But let's face it: the prospect of attending a visioning session is not always greeted with enthusiasm by the conscripts.
>
> We've all been there.
>
> Held captive in a windowless room, hallucinating slowly from a) too much coffee, b) uncapped magic markers, and c) the glaring blankness of the flip charts. We've wordsmithed with a warring group of colleagues well beyond the point of caring. The result is a mission

statement that looked much like our last one—and like everyone else's. Or else we've crafted a vision so lofty, outrageous, or abstract (save the world, conquer the world ...) that seeds of doubt are planted before we leave the room ... Is this really worth the effort?

Jane Logan
Somewhere in Canada

Does this sound familiar? It *should,* because most of us have been through this before. So much so that the organization's mission, vision, and values result in nothing more than words that are hung on a wall somewhere.

To further elaborate on the painful part of the mission and corresponding parts, consider the following true story. We were *not* the consultant in the following illustration.

In a small employer of around one hundred employees, the CEO insisted on mass training, which was done on a quarterly basis. The training usually started on a Friday afternoon and concluded the following Saturday afternoon.

The organization had just gone through a structural change with a transfer from one type of "partnership" into a different form of corporate entity. The CEO felt it was a good time to reexamine the mission of the group. He hired a local consultant he knew to lead the efforts that involved defining a new mission and constructing cascading goals to support the mission. The timing was good. Everyone looked forward to the process.

As usually happens in large training venues, the bigger goal was announced, with several small groups broken out to help construct the new mission. It was a great opportunity to reevaluate and instill a new route to success by totally redefining the organization's mission, vision, and values.

Oh, the best-laid plans of mice and men ... Anyway, the process began.

Because participants were given freedom to argue their point of view, the session went well, until it didn't. The session's leader (aka consultant) found that too much time was being spent on the process of mission redesign. Looking at his watch and at the urging of the CEO, he decided the entire process he was contracted for would be in jeopardy because cascading goals still needed to be written.

His solution was simple. Forget the final version of the mission and get started on writing the goals the organization would follow as a strategy and for the next business plan cycle. That is until someone asked a simple question. How could goals be written if we don't know what our mission truly is?

His answer? We can't hold up the goals process waiting on a final version of the mission!

As a side note, he went home that evening and wrote the new mission for the company, which was lauded by the CEO. Wasted effort, empty words, and no buy-in.

Think about that statement for a few moments. A mission is supposed to be the "North Star," the guidance, yet goals were going to be written around something no one knew anything about.

This is repeated throughout the workforce ... everywhere. Perhaps this is the point to clarify key terms regarding mission, vision, and values. Obviously, there is confusion.

What Is Meant by Mission, Vision, and Values?

Any organization's compass and, therefore, direction should begin with mission, vision, and values. After all, that is the real purpose of the organization's existence. There are various interrelationships between what an organization does and how it behaves as the entity. Therefore, following are simple definitions of each component. These are very succinct pathways that can spell the difference between success and failure.

- A *mission* is the reason for activity. It is *why* we exist.
- A *vision* is the *purpose* we have to carry out our mission and what we want to be.
- A *values statement* is shared beliefs, culture, and *how* we treat ourselves and others in the course of carrying out the organization's mission.

Each of us has at one time or another been involved in the sort of meeting Jane Logan so fluently described. If the feelings expressed by her are valid, then what *is* the point? Of course, it could be the manner in which the meeting was facilitated, but it could also be indicative of the fruitlessness of an exercise that will not change the tenor or the way the organization behaves, in the end. So the question is perhaps this: are mission, vision, and values ever important? If done in the spirit of the intent, then yes.

So this begs the question again. Is there a reason for establishing mission, vision, and values for an organization?

Mission, vision, and values *are* important to the direction of the organization. Without them we are clueless in terms of where we need to go. However, having them, without force behind them ... Well, you get the picture.

In this chapter, we will discover some very important things about an organization's mission, vision, and values and how they can be a driver of success. When constructed correctly, they guide and are a vital part of the organizations systems. When done poorly and without conviction, they become nothing more than meaningless drivel sent from on high and a source of irritation and disenfranchisement from employees.

Let's get started.

Mission, Vision, and Values

Most mission, vision, and values processes begin at the top, and rightfully so. However, they are not a top–down-only document. The development should have involvement from all segments of the organization. A good foundation for developing a strong, useful mission statement begins with leaders asking things such as "What is it about our organization which attracts people to it?" "What do the employees like about what the organization does?" "What is the best thing about our organization when we are functioning in an optimum manner?" "What is the legacy we want to leave behind?" "What contributions do you want to make in a personal sense to the organization?"

These reflective moments require heartfelt dialogue among leaders and each person present speaking to each of these questions, going around until everyone has had an opportunity to capture the essence of the questions above. In truthful dialogue, a pattern of what the organization should be emerges.

As a general guideline, the following items help create a statement that is considered at a minimum "good."

- It is always from deep within and should be purpose driven. It should not include profit motives as a driver. People, including the public, do not equate satisfaction with the need for the organization making money.
- It should appeal to our best interests.
- It is not a generic statement. It must say something that applies to the organization in a unique way.
- It provides direction from year to year and allows discussion, in very specific terms, as to what progress, if any, has been made.
- It has lasting qualities, which means it will be appropriate for years to come and stand the test of time.
- Finally, it has an altruistic tone and nature about it, which means it is for a higher purpose, other than creating income for the organization.

In the meeting used to create or modify the statements, participants must be granted bulletproof status by the organization's leaders, meaning allowed to challenge various concepts. This bulletproof status must extend beyond conference room walls and be exhibited on a daily basis. This helps create the sort of dialogue that fashions and encourages the development of a series of statements that are meaningful. Everyone gets an opportunity to express themselves and the focus should be on supporting, understanding, and clarifying. Dismissing ideas to create shortcuts, rather than exploring the true meaning behind what the person is expressing, must be avoided. As a leader, you must guide this process effectively.

A helpful tip is to look for common themes surrounding what people are saying. These themes can be used as the genesis of the mission, vision, and values of the organization.

Things to avoid include rushing the process, dismissing *any* person's input as insignificant or trivial, along with equating the mission *strictly* with monetary issues. People simply cannot rally around something as sterile as money. Furthermore, anything that focuses on individual endeavors must be avoided. In other words, a mission, vision, and values statement must be selfless for it to be meaningful and able to withstand the test of time and the shift of personalities.

A Process Check

What does a mission, vision, and values statement have to do with running an organization? The answer is simple. These statements become your guidepost to how you will operate and where you will go. In other words, this becomes part of the strategy of the organization. Toward this end, even how the organization handles adversity is impacted by the organization's mission, vision, and values.

Here is a set of circumstances where an organization's mission statement may have saved the entire company. You may be familiar with the story.

Usually, a person can expect one defining moment in their lifetime. James Burke experienced two within six years of each other.

When he was a marketing executive at Johnson & Johnson, he had an overriding sense J&J was getting away from its core values, embodied in their credo established several generations before by one of the founders. In one particularly heated meeting, he boldly proclaimed to the executive team, "Either we live by our credo or we tear it off the wall." In other words, it meant something to him. It's a good thing they kept it, because they would need it six years later when Mr. Burke was the CEO of J&J.

Their credo began with "We believe our first responsibility is to the doctors, nurses, patients, mothers, and fathers who use our products and services."

In October 1982, its credo underwent a crucial test when seven people died after ingesting Tylenol capsules laced with cyanide. When this was discovered, they were faced with a huge dilemma. What to do? As the CEO at this point, James Burke knew. He ordered all products recalled, and all holders of partially used products were provided full refunds. This cost the company one hundred million dollars, a tidy sum in 1982. Its market share dropped 81 percent.

The first instinct was that J&J was committing corporate suicide.

However, as it turned out, this became a textbook example of crisis management, spawned by the belief in its credo, its guiding principles. J&J did the right thing, even at a great loss. Eventually, its market share rebounded and exceeded the original 37 percent of share it previously held. This is a prime example of upholding values as stipulated in a credo. This is the power of an organization's mission, vision, and values.

And James Burke? He was awarded the Presidential Medal of Freedom and was cited by *Fortune Magazine* as one of the ten best CEOs ever.

Now for a contrasting and additional true story. This one too was cyanide poisoning involving product tampering. Once again, the company was not culpable in any fashion. However, the action of one particular location serves as an example of not having appropriate guiding principles.

A news report broadcast the previous evening created a great deal of consternation among leadership at the corporate office as well as satellite operations. A food product made by the company had been tampered with and a consumer subsequently died after ingesting the product laced with cyanide.

It seemed, on the surface, a case of an intentional act of an individual not connected to the operation that manufactured the product.

One of the sister operations which sold their product to plant employees hastily called a meeting of department managers to prepare for local inquiries from the media. Assignments were given on who was to field calls and act as chief spokesperson for the operation. Also, employee product sales were scheduled that week and this meeting was designed to determine what to do about the product sold in the company store. At the meeting, it was not clearly known whether the tampering was widespread or simply a single incident.

Positions were taken by staff managers, with all but one of them in favor of suspending the sale of that particular product until the investigations were over. However, the one not in favor of suspending sales was the person who had overall responsibility for production. And he was adamant, saying, "Products will be sold in the company store; we must protect our brand." His gut feeling was the product-tampering incident was isolated, the risks minimal.

On the other hand, the other managers were fearful that with such news out on the airwaves, if one employee coincidentally contracted even a slight case of indigestion, the company might find itself defending the decision to sell the particular product in the company store. The production head was unbending, but the other company managers were pushing back too. A clear impasse occurred.

The decision on whether or not to pull the stock fell to the operation's general manager, who had absolute and total control and authority over the entire operation.

Both groups turned to him for a final, rightful decision. In a true show of decisiveness, he shrugged his shoulders and slapped the conference room table.

That was it. Meeting over ...

Situations like this occur every day. Some are greater decisions and some are less. Decisions affecting employees, the community, and the organization in particular are heavily influenced by its purpose, its mission, and its values.

Beginning with a Mission Statement

It is not uncommon to hear someone in the midst of an intense moment exclaim, "Look out! I am on a mission!" In fact, this is a sort of statement we may share when we are acting in a determined way. We find ourselves so focused that we are oblivious to anything else around us. It is sometimes used as a way of cautioning people to get out of our way.

When one thinks of a mission statement for an organization, should this not be the basis for the activities that occur within the walls of that company? Yes. As mentioned earlier, a company's mission explains why it exists. Without this foundation, any organization is likely to drift and have no sense of direction.

A mission statement that is written correctly must speak to the business at hand and be written in a very clear and concise manner. It should be written without corporate muckety muck and be such a strong statement that it can stand alone without explanation and be understood.

An example of such a mission statement is that of Starbucks. This mission communicates, loudly and clearly, the task at hand, and you better move out of our way because we are on a mission!

> Our mission: to inspire and nurture the human spirit—
> one person, one cup, and one neighborhood at time.

After reading this statement and experiencing Starbucks' customer service, even during the busiest of times, no one is left to wonder what Starbucks does. There is no further explanation needed as it is simple, concise, and powerful. The only question that may arise is what Starbucks plans to do to accomplish this task and purpose. And this question leads us to the organization's vision.

Having Clear Vision

How comfortable are we finding ourselves driving through thick and sight-impairing fog? Not knowing exactly where you are going, much less what may be in front of you, becomes extremely stressful and creates an almost instant sense of panic. This is the same response organizations set themselves up for by operating with a less than clear and concise vision statement. Vision statements, like mission statements, must not be complicated. Taking something simple and adding complexity sets such a statement up for interpretation.

Your vision statement provides information explaining the future of your company, and quite honestly what your customers or clients can expect from you. It is a statement of purpose explaining what is expected to happen as a result of staying true to the organization's mission. Existing and new businesses alike owe this sense of direction to their employees.

They need to know where they are going and have clarity in order to move forward freely and without hesitation … In other words, without fog.

Below are two vision statement examples written with such clarity and conviction that the entire world knows what they represent. These help define what they will do in order to deliver what their mission statement promises.

A Vision

> To transform communities by inspiring people
> throughout the world to open their minds, accept
> and include people with intellectual disabilities and
> thereby anyone who is perceived as different.
> —Special Olympics

> Ensure that veterans are respected for their service,
> always receive their earned entitlements, and are
> recognized for the sacrifices they and their loved
> ones have made on behalf of this great country.
> —Veterans of Foreign Wars

Considering both organizations are perceived as those embracing diversity and dedication, their vision speaks of extreme clarity of purpose. When an organization has a mission and vision statement everyone understands, there is no need for interpretation. Simple clarity defines an organization's vision. Having a lofty vision does not mean it is unobtainable. It simply means an organization has its eye on the horizon for a greater purpose.

Deeply Seeded Values

Let's first point out that the value statement, if written correctly, should strongly pull an organization toward doing what is right in *any* situation. It must provide a clear understanding of a company's core beliefs and embedded in everything that is done, much like a seed in a flowerbed. Using this correlation, you may begin to form some sort of visual. Maybe your visual is of a beautiful blanket of bluebonnets or an assortment of wild flowers which appear to have been placed with delicate and caring hands. Whatever picture you prefer, there is no arguing the fact that the seeds which were placed there were allowed to flourish. If conditions are not right, seeds do not grow, they may die, and their beauty is never experienced.

A value statement which does not receive attention and frequent revisiting will die much like the seeds that never bloom. A value statement which remains well nourished with activity that reflects its words will result in an organization that blooms with leaders and employees trusting that any decision made will be the right decision. Accordingly, a value statement has a great responsibility. It must keep a company centered without drifting off course. No decision, no matter how large or how small, should be made without holding the group as well as individuals accountable to these words of guidance.

Dan Vasella, former chairman and CEO of Novartis, a global pharmaceutical company, once stated, "Most people have some kind of moral compass that tells them in which direction to go." This is the same moral compass an organization must search for. It must be constructed and communicated in a way that everyone understands.

If, however, a value statement does not clearly communicate the manner in which a company will conduct business, then it is not a good one and leaves far too much room for interpretation and ambiguity. In addition, a value statement that is written *well* but is not reflected in the activity within company walls will breed mistrust and an open invitation to employee disengagement.

Whether an owner, leader, or an employee within an organization, values must be aligned with those of the organization. Without this alignment, there is margin for failure, which may or may not be professional, although most always personal.

Conflicting Priorities

You may not know for certain what your values are until you find yourself under pressure to alter them. Most people have goals and what route is needed to get them achieved. Knowing this seems simple, until something presents itself, which creates a conflict of values. When the values exceed the pursuit of the original goal, sometimes a person stops the chase and examines the cost. For example, Keith Drach.

> While in his early thirties, Drach experienced great success while with General Motors. Being the youngest vice president ever with GM reflects such success. He was on the fast track. He had a personal mission which would surely lead him to the C suite and he would be a part of the rich GM history.
>
> Then it happened. An even more appetizing opportunity presented itself to him. Rather than remain at GM, he left to pursue a new venture. He was named COO of a Silicon

Valley start-up, Qronos Technology. He was destined to be named CEO within a year of his arrival.

What stopped him in his tracks was when he realized success on the fast track proved untenable and in conflict with his personal values. Many fast-track professionals rarely give this a second thought.

In his new role, he discovered the new company did not share his strong sense of values. This mismatch became clear when he was asked to hide issues from the board of directors. This alone painted a much darker picture than what he first perceived. The organization had a mission all right, but their values were simply not in alignment with his moral compass.

Nonetheless, the title of CEO kept driving him forward.

Two core personal values, these being loyalty and integrity, were being challenged, which created significant personal conflict. Even his friends noticed changes in his outward appearance, which appeared to be indicative of anguish.

Then it happened. The defining moment.

As he stood by his wife's side in the middle of her birthing a child, he received an urgent phone call. The message was clear: return to work immediately because a big partner, IBM, was waiting for him. Rather than receiving best wishes on the imminent birth of his child, the message was direct. "We need you here." There was no understanding. The message on the other end smacked of control. This clarified to Drach the value conflict he found himself in.

In a matter of minutes, he made a life-altering decision. He called his boss and simply said, "I quit."

This leads to the following questions.

- Does your company manage by its objectives or values?
- Are your values in line with those of your organization?
- Is there a method in place to be certain that as individuals join the organization their values are in line as well?

The Impact of Living and Breathing One's Mission, Vision, and Values

Each day a leader is faced with opportunities. There are multiple opportunities to interact with staff, customers, and clients and to make decisions similar to those described in this chapter. But what will it take for these impressionable moments, no matter the outcome, to build trust within your organization each and every time?

It is a moment when leadership must do a "checkup from the neck up." It is when a review of communications and decisions are made prior to their implementation to ensure that they speak the same language as the mission, vision, and values of an organization. There is no trust built when a decision is made, or a communication is blasted, if it goes against the values it espouses.

Not only must a leader be extremely familiar with the company's mission, vision, and values, so must each employee—no matter the size of the company or the position the employee occupies. All should be able to express the purpose of each statement as if it were second nature and, if all is done correctly, be able to state how it corresponds to their own values.

Having a clear and concise mission, vision, and value statement is just the beginning. The organization's duty is to assure these beautifully worded and framed plaques come alive and actually mean something to an increasingly diverse workforce.

Chapter 5

Beyond Diversity: Uniting the Workforce

Diversity: the art of thinking independently together
—Malcolm Forbes

As the world got smaller and globalization took hold, people were placed in varying project teams. Demographics began shifting. Organizations found themselves in need of a different sort of training and education.

Even before a smaller world emerged, government programs required inclusion of people previously denied workplace opportunities. A new blended workforce was taking shape. Thus, the concept of diversity was born.

Initially, there was pushback, but over time, a pressing need for skills and experiences required organizations to find ways in which to connect all levels, nationalities, and genders. Immersion training was done on a variety of subjects relating to this, such as harassment. This was originally designed to blend a workforce which allowed workers to pull in one direction for the betterment of the organization.

For those who remember the beginning, diversity training was very instructional. The stated goal was to increase employee awareness, knowledge, and relationship skills. This was done to protect the organization from charges of civil rights violations but to also increase the inclusion of a new diverse group of workers. When performed correctly, even teamwork would be enhanced and promoted.

There is no denying progress was made. However, is the progress enough to allow more diversity as the world of work marches forward? Was the progress made due to training provided or by the natural evolution and gradual acceptance and surrendering of age-old biases? Work and people will continue to be shaped by events that promote and expand opportunities for all regardless of color, religion, age, etc. This is required to be successful in today's world.

However, there is much more work to be done. A new set of steps must be taken. Rather than viewing differences among us, let's look at our similarities.

It is time to look beyond diversity.

What It Is

When asked to identify diversity, a common response is normally, "How we are different." When asked for a deeper explanation, many people provide more wide-ranging responses. One may instantly gravitate toward characteristics that *cannot* be changed. These typically include *race, ethnicity, sex,* and *age.*

However, there are a variety of other types of diversity not commonly associated with the term. These include things that can be changed such as

- education
- work style
- religion
- income
- marital status
- personality

- lifestyle
- culture

Regardless of items that can or cannot be altered, there is a combination of diversity within the workplace. Whenever various factors are considered, the number of seemingly infinite combinations stretches our imagination. Accordingly, a different mind-set with respect to defining diversity emerges.

In addition to the commonly found descriptors of diversity, there may be yet another component. Lying dormant at times, there is a hidden barrier to acceptance that can occur but which rarely gets any attention or is recognized. There are people who, for whatever reason, appear to be a target because people unintentionally have unrecognized biases. These are the blind spots which result in certain individuals becoming easy prey due to the inherent biases most people possess.

Therefore, it is important to know our own blind spots in addition to assisting others in recognizing theirs. This requires leaders to be cognizant and alert for signs of this in others. Signs which indicate resistance to others who happen to have a certain characteristic that brings out the worst in people. This is another one of those issues that plague the workforce and create frustrating issues which management is reluctant to deal with.

When properly managed and actions harnessed in the appropriate way, the employee who may be disenfranchised as being different is protected from harmful effects of unfair treatment. All individuals have biases, and when these biases get out of hand, when they remain unchecked, the workplace suffers. Uncovering these often hidden biases requires honesty and self-reflection. Understanding and preventing hidden predispositions creates a healthy workforce rather than a toxic one. People who are, at a minimum, aware of how they treat people and how their biases stand in the way of fairness can begin to overcome them. This exercise helps preclude them from performing incorrect and even illegal prejudgments.

When considering the multiple facets of diversity and the biases which a leader may or may not be aware of, the risk of an incorrect assessment of resources is real. Organizations unintentionally create yet another barrier, which inhibits growth and opportunity for its workforce. This additional layer of division makes it more difficult to manage what was merely the need to lead multiple cultures, religions, and so forth. Teamwork suffers. So does the bottom line.

Awareness of one's personal biases allows development of a conscious strategy to manage and keep in check emotions thus preventing unnecessary conflict. Recognizing behaviors which create conflict is a critical and important step toward increasing understanding of others. Ultimately, and if handled properly, this recognition will improve interaction among all stakeholders within the organization.

Knowing what diversity is and how it is complicated with personal biases is important. However, using the knowledge gained in a positive way is crucial in setting the stage for promising future outcomes.

Popular Diversity

A diversity issue that gets a lot of attention today in blogs, articles, and research is a current one which most recognize, yet do not seem to have a handle on ... generational diversity. This topic quickly formulates its own sort of negative branding and target even before a person says anything. This adds unnecessary complications by labeling groups and then proclaiming a generation gap exists.

Of course, there is a need to understand how generations differ. However, it is vitally important to go beyond a label and learn what positive attributes various generations possess. In fact, generational differences should be utilized primarily for understanding *possible* strengths rather than how each generation is simply different. A group working together, from multiple generations, requires the evolved leader to understand and share knowledge of all team members in order to strengthen the work group.

Recognizing people as individuals and acknowledging their contributions enables others to view things through a new prism.

The following chart illustrates accepted generational differences along with the skill set each group possesses. It must be noted there is nothing on the chart which indicates the absence of wanting to work. The chart simply illustrates how results are obtained. Moreover, each generation currently in the workforce, including the upcoming ones, can actually learn from each other. There should never be any roadblocks to learning, regardless of generation.

Generation	Key attributes
Traditionalists (to 1945)	Hardworking. Puts own needs aside and believes that if they do this they will get the job done. A reward for them is hard work and the greatest gift they have for the workforce is their mentoring and teaching.

Baby Boomers (1946–1964)	Workaholic. Struggle for time for self since they are sandwiched between home and work demands, volunteering, and social events. Burnout is real. This generation strives to make an impact and is asking, "What about me?"
Generation X (1965–1980)	Only work as hard as needed, but in a good way. Their goal is to work smart. Looking to change things that are already in place by using technology. They have fresh eyes and question things that have been in place for a long time. Not very trusting and push back to keep a work/life balance that the baby boomers did not have. Want to continue to grow and learn. Love projects, and if given one, they love to run with it. Also believe that they have a better chance of seeing a UFO than a social security check in their lifetime.
Generation Y or Millennials (1981–2000)	Most digital generation and wants to be in a caring profession. Wants to do something that will make a difference. If they leave a position, it is because they didn't feel like they fit in. Often need to be eased into receiving constructive criticism due to their upbringing. This is the group where self-evaluations truly come in handy.
Generation Z or Digital Natives (2000–2010)	Extremely comfortable and even dependent on technology. Multitasking gurus using a variety of online products and sophisticated electronic devices, with an appreciation for simple, interactive designs. Socially responsible. Always connected, making networking across countries and cultures second nature. This connectedness will influence their decision-making process.

What's next ... **Generation A or** **Alpha (2010–)**	Time will tell what this generation will bring to the table. Preliminary reports predict an extremely technologic, efficient, and savvy group of workers. A majority of their toys were either electric or battery driven, rather than mechanical. Technology surrounds them.

Information found in the chart is helpful, but it is not definitive. While important, it does not establish total value each group brings to or passes on to other generations. The leader is still required to understand values of each generation of workers. Rather than stereotyping any group, the evolved leader will explore the many advantages of the diversity they encounter.

Consider the following.

An airplane conversation between an HR manager and an MIT student ensues. The HR manager learned the student was a double major in engineering and just finished a summer internship with a prestigious oil and gas company.

When the student was asked how she liked the internship, she responded that it was okay, but she had found it difficult to work within the group she was assigned. Naturally curious, the manager asked why and was told she was assigned a task of implementing a new process and received a great deal of pushback from a senior-level engineer who thought the process simply wouldn't work. The manager then pressed for how long the senior engineer had been employed at the company, whereupon the student rolled her eyes and said, "Forever." After confirming the engineer was indeed "senior," the manager asked this highly educated, motivated, and promising student if she had ever asked for advice or even help from the older worker in terms of the new process. The student responded she had not.

To her credit, the student realized that her time at the company would have been better served had she understood the dynamics of the department she was assigned to. She also realized that although she knew how to get from point A to point B, she had forgotten to bring along and include the senior employee who was going to have to live with the new process long after she was gone.

She attributed the failure to an older mind-set when in reality she had failed to include in the mix, one of the people most affected by the change.

This requires each of us to dig deeper. After all, motivators are basically the same regardless of the generational divide, if there is actually a divide. Instead of managing individuals by generation, the smart leader uses the skills each group possesses. In normal social settings, which includes work, people generally respond to the culture which is prevalent.

For this reason, cross training needs to be utilized between the generations. Learning, understanding, and accepting the value of this model is vitally important. This needs to happen quickly too. There are two generations which will be leaving the workforce soon.

Irrespective of the generation, leadership is needed. This further enables an employee fulfillment in their jobs today and development in their jobs now and in the long term.

A Compelling Reason for Embracing Diversity

Industry in the twenty-first century has changed in many ways. There is nothing to indicate the constantly changing work environment will slow down any time soon. While some businesses operate solely on the premise of utilizing modern technology, others still rely heavily on labor-intensive strategies. Further clouding the landscape is the notion of working for one company during an entire career is no longer an expectation of the younger generation.

Every employee who leaves the organization takes with them their knowledge, relationship building skills, and their contributions. Potential problems arising from labor shortages raise questions about the effects of the expectations of succeeding generations on employer economics. Other questions concern where additional shortages in the labor market may occur and the effects of the global economy has on labor needs in the United States.

It is increasingly difficult for employers in certain industries to find, place, and retain workers necessary in keeping the United States competitive with the rest of the world. This has far-reaching consequences for this country, its people, its national well-being, and the various infrastructures supported by a sound and vibrant economy. The problem is simplistic in its nature, that being finding and retaining a workforce. However, it is highly complex in its solution and transcends government, systems, economies, and the well-being of future generations.

Many issues surround this challenge. The new generations will have higher expectations as they enter the workforce. These expectations are based on the educational level as well as technological advances. Today students are taught at early ages the importance of technology. Early computer classes, video games, and the Internet have created a technologically advanced generation as compared to the previous baby boomer and traditionalist ones.

There are additional concerns. The traditional population growth of native-born American citizens is slowing down. Beginning in 2010, this segment of population grew by only 3 percent, and by 2030, it will be down to only 1.1 percent annually. The real gap involves selected skills, not head counts. The question is not whether there will be enough workers, but whether there will be enough *qualified* workers on US soil to do the work at an acceptable cost.

In the past, people would work for a corporation until retirement age. It was a different time, without the competitive global economy, and without the technologically advanced generations that have evolved. *The US Department of Labor: Workforce 2000 Facts* stated the following:

1. The average person in the United States holds 9.2 jobs between age eighteen and thirty-four.
2. More than *half* of these jobs are held by people between the ages of eighteen and twenty-four.

These two issues alone cause churn.

Today, organizations must be cognizant of impending labor shortages in the United States, which are caused by a multitude of factors.

A large group of skilled workers will be lost with the retirements of the baby boomer generation. Shortages in skilled labor and skilled trades in particular, such as heavy equipment mechanics, operators, construction workers, and truck drivers, could affect the way organizations do business. Some statistics report that native-born baby boomers account for almost half of the current US workforce.

With the older sector of baby boomers retiring, the United States will begin to see a shortage of skilled workers. The younger generations, X and Y, have higher expectations toward seeking jobs with the technological skills and college education to back their expectations. They may not be interested in craftsmanship jobs that require getting their hands dirty or working outside. This raises the question of who will build houses, fix cars, and build roads and bridges.

Employers must begin preparing different ways to maintain an adequate employee base and develop strategic elements to hiring practices as well as retention ones. These must be developed through competitive benefit and compensation structures, as well as a corporate structure, which satisfies and maintains employees. A well-defined and inclusive corporate culture is of paramount importance and will assist in alleviating hiring and retention of the workforce.

In years past, the immigrant population helped the United States with providing workers for craftsmanship jobs. Today, with the focus on immigration, that may not be the case. The aftermath of 9/11 affected the ability of immigrant populations requesting educational visas to receive them and has affected the status of immigrant populations from bordering countries such as Mexico and other Latin American countries. These immigrants have filled jobs that American young adults or generation Y are not interested in pursuing. If they are unable to migrate to the

United States to fill these jobs, industry such as construction will have difficulty finding workers.

The number of Hispanics in the workforce increased by 659,641 in one year alone, ten years ago. The construction industry was responsible for more than half of total Hispanic job gains. The construction industry had been facing substantial labor shortages, and the influx of Latino workers became a key factor in helping builders meet the increasing demand for housing and commercial construction.

Another reason for the labor shortage in the United States is the anticipated decline in the native-born US workforce.

The birthrate in the United States started rapidly declining in the 1970s. Presently, the rate has reached a point where the economy may be affected by it. This will cause, for the first time in US history, a workforce that retracts. The United States experienced a 12 percent decline in the thirty-five- to forty-four-year age segment and a 3 percent decline in the thirty to thirty-four year age group at the close of the last decade. Unless there is another dramatic increase through immigration, there will be at least five million *fewer* workers ages thirty to forty-four than there are now.

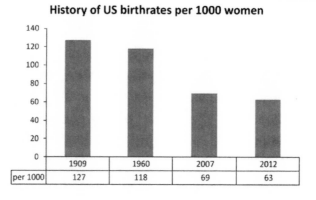

History of US birthrates per 1000 women

	1909	1960	2007	2012
per 1000	127	118	69	63

Evidence *once* existed which suggested there were no imminent concerns about labor shortages. American businesses eliminated workers from their payrolls through various mergers, acquisitions, and job exportation to countries such as India. However, this proved wrong. There are currently three million more job openings than there are workers to fill them.

Of course, some labor demands have been filled by nontraditional sources, such as women and Hispanics; however, these sources alone cannot fill the positions vacuum created by the retirement of the baby boom generation. Accordingly, the organization's culture, advancement opportunities, and acceptance of diversity all play a key role in both attracting and retaining workers.

Behaviors Adopted and Publicized

The preceding information makes a strong case of not only understanding diversity but also applying it to the workforce.

To begin managing diversity, leadership must understand and implement a strategy for leading a diverse workforce. This requires acceptance by stakeholders and encouragement of principles within work teams. Studies indicate that managing a diverse workforce contributes to increased staff retention and productivity. It also helps enhance an organization's responsiveness to an increasingly diverse world of customers and improves relations with the surrounding community. This helps increase the organization's ability to cope with change and expand the innovation and creativity within the organization. Furthermore, a strategy for training both managers and staff on how to work effectively in a diverse environment prevents discrimination and promotes inclusiveness.

All these factors lend credence to a healthier work environment and increased buy-in by internal as well as external stakeholders, including the end customer.

However, acceptance and encouragement related to this training and education also reinforces sound leadership and helps preclude involvement of third-party interference brought on through issues such as racism, sexism, ageism, cultural differences, class distinctions, religion, and sexual preference. In addition, diversity also demonstrates good faith to employees, government, and potential clientele. It establishes a premise of acceptance and intolerance of any form of discrimination. An organization which trains and educates along the lines of diversity helps influence behaviors of the workforce, who outwardly convey positive feedback to the community as well as consumers. With the advancement of rapid communications found in social media, organizations cannot afford to project incongruent images. Simply put, negative comments will be found on Twitter, Instagram, Facebook, and other public forums.

Additionally, training and education receives an extra boost of *we are serious* by instituting robust policies which deliver salient messages of accepting the diversity that surrounds each of us. Engaging such policies and embracing education of them enables an organization to protect itself against poor public relations perception, lawsuits, loss of business, and more importantly, loss of good people.

Over the years, many organizations have enhanced their practices by instituting steps which lead to positive outcomes before it was considered in vogue. On the other hand, other organizations have had to deal with fallout from failure to do the right thing. A sound and well-executed diversity program has a goal of providing an environment where all are allowed to excel and where people's talents, ideas, and involvement create a harmonious culture. A diversity program also helps meet legal requirements, and these are in abundance everywhere, from local ordinances to state and federal government.

A Watchful Eye

As previously illustrated, new technologies, population shifts, and shrinking global barriers have rapidly changed the dynamics of diversity. Employment opportunities are now available for previously excluded members of society. There is a fundamental need to responsibly recruit and manage workers previously denied opportunities regardless of preconceived biases or diverse background.

These factors alone make diversity, culture, and inclusion vitally necessary to the workforce of today and tomorrow. These should also encourage an organization to do the right thing and utilize the talent that lies before them. However, not every organization has deep value systems which would encourage doing the right thing. Therefore, legislation, both state and federal, was passed and made into law, which addressed systemic inequities which stemmed from poor organizational convictions.

Accordingly, key laws were developed to keep a watchful eye on circumstances and to assure that diversity in general was not ignored. Organizations became familiar with the pertinent antidiscrimination laws as a result of barriers which existed in the workforce of yesteryear.

Unfortunately, compliance did not necessarily guarantee inclusion but at least provided an essential floor for previously denied groups to be recognized and advanced. Laws, such as the Equal Pay Act of 1963, Age Discrimination in Employment Act of 1967, Americans with Disabilities Act (ADA), and the Civil Rights Act of 1964 (as amended) all called attention to the fact that employers practices were being monitored and compliance to the statutes required.

The Equal Employment Opportunity Commission (EEOC) is charged with assuring a discrimination-free work environment exists. It investigates and attempts to mitigate discrimination for women and minorities through equal employment opportunities without regard to race, color, religion, disability, gender, or national origin. It is also responsible for investigating age discrimination claims. All these create at least a baseline for inclusion.

While not designed to discredit the efforts of government to promote diversity, the concept of compliance unfortunately creates an element of control through regulation and reporting requirements. These efforts may have brought this subject to the forefront, but that *deeper* understanding of one another may not have been the result. Chances are little sincere and complete change in the acceptance of diversity occurs when enforcement is the driver.

Even though compliance may meet legal needs, it does not necessarily meet the needs of the people. Some organizations recognize this and are listening to their workforce. For example, large corporations, such as Disney and Boeing, are leading the way in various cutting-edge concepts. These two companies, and many others, are offering gender-neutral benefits such as health insurance to unmarried domestic partners, which it provides to more traditional spousal arrangements. This treatment reflects the view that all employee groups deserve the right to work in an environment that is nondiscriminatory. In addition, policies of this nature are forward thinking by not excluding groups based on their set of diversity or a leader's personal bias.

Daniel Pink, in his landmark book *Drive,* illustrates this best by stating, "People might meet the minimal ethical standards to avoid punishment, but the guidelines have done nothing to inject purpose into the corporate bloodstream." Accordingly, diversity acceptance is more than just an exercise where the organization fills in a series of boxes and verifies its actions. It requires a commitment to increase the acceptance of it.

Stagnant Focus

Laws, policies, and training keep us focused on diversity, culture, and inclusion. Much work and effort goes into identifying differences, but little goes into why behaviors and actions exist. The manner which encourages and embraces a diverse and culturally aligned workforce, irrespective of differences, is proven to be the linchpin for twenty-first-century organizations.

Identifying and then putting labels on individuals in the workplace breeds resentment and, worse, negates the possibility of working together in a seamless manner. Working around others who are not accepted as mainstream creates one additional barrier which separates the workforce instead of joining forces and pulling in one direction. When barriers are created between generations, as well as other types of diversity, there is a possibility of real loss that is not found on corporate financial statements.

There have been great strides in learning and understanding how people are different. However, it is not until the focus of differences is removed and then replaced with a common focus and common goals will true diversity become accepted. When this is done and made part of the makeup of the organization, all will be able to capitalize on the great strengths of the whole.

A good example of this is found in every Olympiad. Each four years, a group of gifted, talented, and hardworking athletes ascend on the games they participate in. They attend with enthusiasm and desire to compete on a world stage. This is perhaps the greatest assemblage of diversity known in the world. During the summer games, 10,500+ athletes from almost every country in the world focus on the approaching competition.

These athletes pull together and in one direction. Of course, they have a common goal: to make it to the Olympics and to do well and bring home the gold. We should learn from this group of aspiring athletes and maybe this is the type of goal leaders should aspire to replicate in their own work teams. The leader must communicate a goal that is clear, concise, and account for all team members adding value. They need to focus on this commonality rather than on the team's differences and bring the spirit of the Olympics to the workplace.

On a much smaller scale, the workplace experiences the challenge of addressing multiple focuses every day. It may be due to the fact that emphasis is incorrectly placed on differences, rather than how people are the same. A leader may use the Olympics as a guide to establishing a workforce of unity rather than separation.

One concept which may provide clarity is found in the following illustration. This is an example of two things. First, how a leader alters the tone for the work group. And second, how the work group responds. Both exemplify a new focus which enhances our ability to make work inclusive, dynamic, and rewarding. Plus the unique approach described below alleviated a particular organization's revolving door, which is commonly found in third-shift operations.

> A night-shift supervisor looks out on the production floor and notes an unusual silence. The normal din of machinery and shouts were replaced by an eerie quietness.
>
> With a bit of trepidation, the supervisor proceeded to investigate the situation by stepping out of his office to check it out. What he discovered was something very encouraging to him. There was dialogue taking place between his staff and a new employee. This important conversation, which normally took place between the supervisor and new staff member, was being conducted by his own team. What a proud moment for this supervisor.
>
> The conversation was a result of a practice he encouraged and spearheaded. Now it was being adopted by his team. During the new employee's first critical day, special attention was devoted to get to know and understand the newest member.
>
> An onboarding process, which he developed and instituted on his own, was done so sincerely and candidly that the process enabled discussion of every individual's needs, as well as needs of the team. This was done by collecting information and encouraging dialogue regarding an individual's diverse background, values, and desired development.

The culture he established, and the employees embraced, was unique. Instead of nervously welcoming individuals with a diverse background, a level of comfort was quickly established.

As a result of sound communications in an open environment, conversations became very natural and without judgment. This open dialogue created a new understanding among employees.

This department set a best practice for the organization. Employees became well versed on the diversity within the company—so much so that they wanted to share their wealth of knowledge with their community. One such activity, sponsored by the establishment but coordinated solely by employees, was the creation of cultural cookbooks to share. They were originally destined to be separate cultural "cookbooks" until the employees decided it would be only one cookbook with culturally diverse recipes.

This was to signify that they were a united group with one common goal ... to bring good food to the table.

Who could argue with that?

Adopting a New Behavior

Now is the time to view diversity through an entirely different lens. This new lens strips away the essence of some of our old leadership DNA and focuses on things that really matter. Important and enlightening characteristics, such as values and goals, along with understanding of how we can become loyal and supportive colleagues, need to become the new lunchroom dialogue.

This must begin with leadership. As leadership continues on their diversity path, they must intertwine a communications plan encompassing a new view. Open dialogue is not fostered by reading a book about diversity. Where it begins is by sharing, inquiring, and understanding. An open dialogue chips away at the barriers which may have been allowed within an organization. Once mutual and common values are uncovered, an engaged workforce emerges.

You cannot lead people until you know them, and people won't follow you until they know and trust you.

However, any leader who feels uncomfortable when dealing with a diverse work group will create an atmosphere which diminishes creativity and contributions from many people. When creativity is unleashed, a sound culture and work environment develops. Where a positive, inclusive environment emerges, breakthrough performance follows. Of course, this takes time. It takes education, training, and clear communications, along with behaviors which match the message, to make this a reality.

Diverse Teams

Diversity is here to stay. Some employers have already started to recognize the need for real and open dialogue to take place, as described in the story previously shared. However, this is not happening enough. There are leaders who continue have an impenetrable wall when faced with what they consider the challenge of working with individuals from a diverse background.

These same leaders prevent open dialogue from happening freely and frequently enough.

It is imperative that leaders understand how to communicate as well as behave in a way that encourages conversation rather than relying solely on the instructional diversity training many organizations are accustomed to. Open dialogue, led by leaders, will encourage a more thorough understanding of one another.

For a team to successfully work together in either a departmental sense or on a specific project, the time spent to lay a good foundation before expectations are communicated is vitally important. There must be a clearly defined and communicated charter for project teams, and there must be an understanding of one another. This understanding includes, but is not limited to, knowing one another's work habits and styles, preferred hours of work, and day-to-day schedules (especially if a team consists of individuals working from a variety of locations). Once everyone is on the same page with regard to expectations for the project and deadlines, as well as understanding team members' values, then a new sort of team emerges. The team will be poised for success by displaying effective teamwork and a strong sense of camaraderie.

Leaders who have managed teams in the past know from experience that the initial outcome is not always pleasant. Because of this, a leader must be present to provide guidance and offer delicate reminders along the way to prevent internal team competition. Team members may need to be reminded to be watchful for how they treat others. Particular attention will need to be shown to prevent resentful feelings caused by individuals pushing too hard. In addition, blind spots should be addressed, as they are observed to prevent unwarranted discord.

Bringing together a qualified group of individuals to create a team or complete a project is the easy part. Guiding that team through the struggles associated with diversity is not. However, the more ingrained this new view of diversity becomes, the easier it is for all to accept and embrace.

A Final Check

Leaders must encourage and demonstrate the recognition of similarities rather than differences. This can be effectively done with the sort of open dialogue advocated in this chapter. This communication will lead you to a better understanding of the values and needs of those you work with and help you identify their strengths. A leader will identify and promote the strength of their employees and the organization.

The commitment to a new behavior which encourages this never-ending pursuit of open dialogue should become a permanent and integral part of an organization's mission, vision, and value statement. In addition, the actions within an organization, especially those demonstrated by leadership, must consistently reflect the words written for all to follow.

Understanding the many trials associated with demographic changes and then incorporating a new path which accepts more inclusion, better communications, and diversity fortifies an organization now and well into the future. This new path helps strengthen all segments of the organization and society as a whole.

Organizations must not hesitate to evolve. They must constantly evaluate those threats that create barriers and prevent utilization of people's talents. This leads to success and a win-win for all concerned.

Continuously improving the organization's understanding of diversity, liberating those differences, and focusing on how we are the same removes barriers. Consequently, organizations are in a better position to create an environment attractive to the evolved workforce. This new environment places any business ahead of the competition. Once an organization is fully onboard with a new view of diversity, new talent will be enticed to join the team, regardless of tight labor markets. They will be excited to experience this new culture you have created.

The benefits are many, and the time is now. However, even with the best intentions, there are still times when people simply don't get along and conflict inhibits progress. Evolved organizations have methods to deal with these issues quickly and effectively.

This is covered next.

Chapter 6

The Triangle with More Than Three Sides: Removing Internal Conflicts That Inhibit Progress

In the middle of every difficulty, lies opportunity.
—Albert Einstein

Embracing the day with an action plan is not uncommon. It keeps us on task and is designed to assure those things that are important are accomplished. Unfortunately, without warning, plans often change. An urgent matter involving some type of conflict occurs which needs our guidance.

This is an all too familiar reality for individuals who occupy a leadership role. If it's not familiar, things may be occurring behind the scenes which you have no knowledge of. The flow of information could be choked off before it ever reaches you and underground conflicts may be undermining your team. In either case, negative conflicts damage both the organization and its people.

The most aggravating and perplexing problems organizations encounter involve conflict among workers. Conflict occurs among spouses, family, and friends. There is a strong likelihood it will occur in a work setting too.

Negative conflicts are unhealthy for any organization. If not dealt with effectively and timely, they fester, grow, and become almost too big to handle. Furthermore, any type of conflict, both negative and constructive, needs a channel to effectively resolve the issue(s). However, in terms of resolution, promoting indiscriminate use of discipline, control or even threats of retaliation are not healthy either. A solution that is clear, which comes from leadership, fosters a set of behaviors that are easily recognizable by anyone connected to the organization.

Standards of behaviors outlined in an organization's well-written and supported mission, vision, and values provide the impetus for sound communications. But human nature oftentimes interferes with this. A cornerstone of leadership is building a culture where values are maintained and conflict becomes something that results in learning rather than disruption. Communicating and living the right message allows for easier and more productive solutions to conflicts when they arise.

Nonetheless, the evolved leader must be prepared for the inevitable negative conflict.

Why Conflict Exists

There are probably very few who can attest to never having been a victim of negative conflict, whatever the form. Unfortunately, some people seem to be plagued by receiving what is perceived as more than their fair share of bullying, gossip, and/or triangulation.

If behaviors such as these are so painful, hurtful, and bad for business, why does it continue? Why does it infiltrate every level of an organization? The reasons may be numerous, but let's dissect a few to determine the root cause found in this abnormal, peculiar, yet all too familiar behavior that affects many organizations.

First, managers and leaders must not only be able to identify the various and sundry types of conflict but also understand why they exist. Then an organization can organize their efforts in achieving an environment where everyone encourages and embraces only those behaviors that enhance an organization.

One explanation could be associated with one's own shortcomings. To combat this, and thereby make themselves feel superior, they thrive on making others feel inferior. When a person is feeling down, they may find a boost by someone else being in a worse situation than they are. If this opportunity doesn't exist, and a victim is not readily available, they will seek out one and simply make something up. Or at least try.

Another poor behavior may stem from wanting to be part of a larger group. If a person perceives success by way of engaging in gossip and rumors as witnessed by others, there is a tendency to contribute something to feel inclusive. Unfortunately, the person on the down side of the gossip is typically the one left out, powerless to do anything about it at the moment. Most of us, at some point, have been caught up in this cycle, which is malicious and contrary to accepted societal values. However, it happens in the nation's capital, state capitals, work, and even homes.

Seeking attention, whether positive or negative, does not change once adulthood is reached. If you are the first person to hear something important, it is akin to finding free money. Whether it's true or not, you feel like you possess something everyone else wants and no one else has. So human nature has us take advantage of that situation and buy that attention for as long as possible. This is done by holding out until the perfect moment and then blurting out the important information which only you hold in the palm of your hand or on the tip of your tongue.

Perhaps this is a way of gaining some semblance of control. Whereas bad conflict creates ill will, control ultimately weakens an organization. Previous teachings indicated a need for leadership to be in control. This is misguided in today's world. It is true people like control, but they don't like being controlled. Control in this context simply means "in order." Unfortunately, for generations, control has been a disruptive yet under the radar behavior.

Another control issue is simple jealousy. Jealousy is not attractive on anyone, and in the world of conflict, this is no exception. Being jealous of an individual often has a tendency to lead to rumors. People get hurt in the process. Or a person may feel hurt by the popularity or admiration another person receives. Instead of celebrating their success, jealousy becomes the behavior of choice. You get an overwhelming urge to heap revenge on the other person, in order to beat the competition down.

Lastly, often people begin a rumor simply due to boredom!

Studies have indicated that boredom is the number one reason for creating rumors. Unfortunately, some people are simply not happy unless there is grumbling or uneasiness. When things become too quiet, they create phantom issues. A great example of this is the popularity of Hollywood gossip. In fact, there is an entire industry dedicated to this concept of spreading rumors. Tabloids and Internet gossip are exploitive and unfortunately accepted as a form of entertainment.

Without understanding the detriments of conflict and control along with why they take place, efforts to deal with various forms of conflict prove difficult. However, when conflict is dismantled brick by brick, leadership clearly and succinctly demonstrates it is no longer welcome in the workplace, home, or society.

Let's assure negative conflict no longer has a purpose.

Triangulation and Conflict

Before a simple and effective method of handling conflict is unveiled, you need to be able to identify the many faces of conflict. Conflict is usually much more than normally meets the eye. Oftentimes, there are deeply hidden emotions and strong undercurrents that are not easily detected. Although management and leadership spend too much of their work time dealing with these issues, many look upon it as an accepted ritual. Time is too valuable to reside in this world.

Abetting these issues which feed nearly every type of conflict is a term called *triangulation*.

For this reason, triangulation is one of the more difficult to resolve but also one that can be extinguished if employees are taught to identify and deal with it. In simple terms, a triangulation event occurs when a person not involved in a particular conflict is brought into the mix. Rather than facing one set of distressing circumstances between two people, triangulation adds three, four, or even more individuals to the struggle. No matter what type of conflict you are dealing with, they all contribute to disruption in the workday and ultimately affect workflow, morale, and organizational effectiveness.

The following cause and effect chart helps illustrate workplace behaviors which surface on any given day. Many of them go underground, making you unaware of the long-term effects.

These are the most common issues organizations face, which eventually lead to triangulation issues.

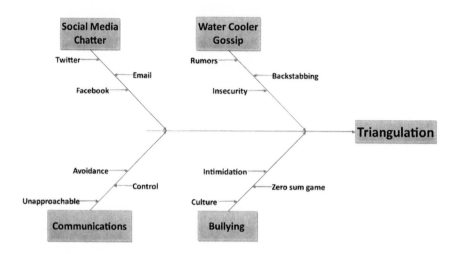

These behaviors typically get addressed by human resources and leadership in the form of policies. These policies are designed to discourage objectionable behavior and have the ultimate goal of protecting employees from this continuing in the workplace. Corporate America does not seem to have a very good handle on the situation. Typically, policies are written to address situations in a negative manner, which lends to mistrust at the onset, even to the most trustworthy employee. They are often inconsistently followed and many times poorly documented. Additionally, when written, rather than creating open healthy dialogue between management and employees, they instill fear. Instead of encouraging communication and understanding of policies, they often instill a culprit mentality in the minds of employees.

As an illustration, let's examine a common and timely issue surrounding the use of social media and the communication policy conundrum.

Social media. Modern communication vehicles, such as Twitter, e-mail, Facebook, and Instagram—there are many, many more—have enabled negative conflicts to go viral. Social media has provided those who wish to provoke issues one more and one very efficient way of doing just that. Whether the intentions are used in a way to gossip, bully, spread rumors about someone, or innocently used as an effective way of staying in touch with friends, relatives, and business acquaintances, employers are on the lookout. The policies and resulting technology fixes work overtime to keep this potential abuse under control.

Unfortunately, an unnecessary element of fear from both management and their employees dominates the workplace whenever tactics such as these are utilized. Even the ones who use devices for the most appropriate purposes do so at great peril. To prevent misuse of this tool, a universal procedure promulgated by the organization is instituted. Usually, this process prevents its use in its entirety. For example a particular company had a strict policy pertaining to Internet use. It employed Internet-tracking software to monitor Internet traffic. One day, after the tracking report came out, an employee was tagged as an abuser and accused of surfing the Internet, rather than performing her assigned duties.

As it turned out, the abuse was baseless. The Internet usage traced to her desk was not abusive at all. She had simply been listening to Internet radio at her desk. No one informed the so-called "abuser" that this would cause issues, so a judgment was made. In this case, not only was an innocent individual made to feel like a criminal, but she also was tracked taking advantage of a piece of technology (listening to the radio). The company did not have a policy prohibiting the use of the Internet for this particular purpose and lumped all Internet usage into one category.

Many times those who are otherwise responsible and trustworthy when using available technology are almost forced to violate the policy. However, there may be a very real need to obtain important information in a timely manner, resulting in the innocuous use of such a tool.

Here is another instance regarding social media and timely communications. Many school districts utilize texting as a way to communicate with parents, both working and nonworking. The important communication is sent to a smart phone alerting them of inclement weather, forced school closings, and other school-related issues. However, in today's workplace, you find that having one's cell phone at their desk may be prohibited per company policy. This, without a doubt, is a very good example of outdated organization policies. This is due to reluctance of losing control. Rather than embracing fast technology and communications, there is lack of trust from leadership.

A better solution would be to embrace the technology and prohibit the bad behavior. After all, aren't many companies now using Facebook and Twitter as a form of advertising and maintaining a presence through these means?

Let's look at defining additional issues organizations encounter that impede the journey to employee engagement and sound organizational practices.

Water cooler gossip (or coffee klatch chatter). This is that moment in time when one person passes on information in its entirety or as a partial tidbit hoping to spark interest from the listener. Once an individual's attention is captured, the gossiper tends to take advantage of this opportunity by providing as much information as possible, whether true or not, to make the stop well worth it to the listener.

The speaker often adopts a confidential tone and is using the information about somebody else to be the center of attention and will impart the details in a way that tries to undermine the credibility or likability of another person. The details may be given with moralizing undertones, and character assassination may be the top of the gossiper's agenda. Often people are told many more personal details than one cares to know about. The motivations behind gossip include attention-seeking, self-inflation, exaggeration, and a "me versus them" mentality.

There are many more forms of gossip, including using the grapevine. This pertains to general change occurring within a workplace. Someone started it and now it is running about like an uncontrolled fire. Usually, this happens in an uncertain environment and is fueled by fear, poor communications from management levels, and wild guesses by staff. It is less personal than gossip attacking another person but is as equally damaging and demoralizing.

The goal is simple. This behavior is designed to have this news catch like wildfire (the rumor state), make someone look like the bad guy even though their efforts were superior (backstabbing state), or simply make them feel better during their day by passing on information which makes them look on top of their game (insecurity).

Communications. There are workplaces which boast of having a wonderful, dynamic communications method in place. As a result, leadership is confident that any internal conflict will be taken care of as a result of the culture they have developed.

What organizations may not realize, however, are the effects pertaining to how the communication plan is expressed to its people. If the plan is not executed with genuineness as its core, and if the behaviors of the individual promoting the communication vehicle do not match, the message becomes essentially worthless.

For instance, a leader who publicly pronounces they are approachable, the door is always open, etc. and then closes off their communication sends a poorly contrived and mixed signal. They have set the stage for employee disenchantment. Employees simply tune the insincere initial message out. Such behavior creates an environment ripe for the origins of conflict. Mixed communication signals contribute to inevitable conflict by creating false expectations rather than clear, honest, and direct dialogue.

Here is an example of an open-door promise that went awry.

> A seasoned corporate manager changed jobs and joined a different company. After the usual hullabaloo associated with the interview, vetting, and job offer, the manager was hired by a director of a particular operation. After settling in his new office, he had not paid attention to a critical item. Although the director seemed outgoing, welcoming, and genuinely pleased he had joined his team, the new manager was stunned on his first day of the new job.

> It seems the open-door policy, working closely together, and so forth he had been promised vanished. Whenever

the manager needed to visit his director, he first had to view a set of lights above the director's door. A green light signified, "Come in," while a red light indicated, "Stay away, and don't disturb me."

The open-door policy was not so "open" after all.

Bullying. A young person takes their life because they were subjected to extreme bullying by way of direct contact or social media. Then, after all is said and done, those knowing the deceased reflect on the fact that they did not have any idea this was transpiring. Bullying is not confined to the schoolyard anymore. It happens in the workplace too. Bullying may be occurring right in front of your eyes through intimidation, by the culture allowed, by leadership's non-involvement, and by those who are firm believers in zero-sum game.

Bullying is a systematic campaign of interpersonal destruction that jeopardizes a person's health, career, and, many times, the job once loved. Bullying can be physical, but the less obvious and just as destructive, is the non-physical type of bullying. Though not physical it is still abusive and emotional harm frequently results.

In a normal sense, a person who is bullied does not set about being the object of this behavior. Bullying in the workplace is not illegal, yet it's about four times more common than either sexual harassment or racial discrimination on the job.

Unfortunately, most people cannot confront the bully. If so, it would have been taken care of. The concept of bullying is unhealthy, destructive, and hampers solid, fruitful communications most organizations strive for.

There are no statutes presently found in any US state that prohibit this behavior. There are no laws. It is up to leadership to confront and deal with this contemporary issue that causes so much workplace harm.

Revisiting triangulation. As mentioned, triangulation occurs whenever a person, rather than addressing the conflict directly with an individual, opts for a different approach. A third party (and sometimes many more) becomes involved. To give you a better idea of how this complicates things, the following is a situation from a few years ago.

Can you discern the difficulties which surrounded this particular situation?

> A human resources manager is approached by two individuals from the same department within a large retail store. The purpose of their visit was to inform the manager of a third person in their department who smelled poorly. They are offended by their coworker's odor and have talked to others. Everyone agrees this person basically stinks.
>
> The HR manager calls in the employee who has just had a complaint lodged against them. The manager does not smell anything offensive but needs to address the issue with the employee. As a result, the manager provides the standard message. "I don't smell anything, but I have received complaints from individuals in your department who indicate you may have an odor problem. Please review your hygiene practices to ensure this does not continue or you will be subject to discipline up to

and including termination of your employment per the employee handbook."

The employee quit their job immediately. They were unable to face the embarrassment of going back to the department.

This particular story has a number of missteps. The first was it just so happened that the two employees who did the reporting to HR did not like the person they complained about. They cooked up a scheme to get rid of the employee by starting a rumor, which they surmised (correctly) would be addressed by management. Secondly, they knew their coworker was a very sensitive person. They understood that when the issue was addressed, the coworker would probably quit. They were correct once again.

Wouldn't you rather be told directly from one person that you may have an odor problem rather than be talked about behind your back or—worse yet—have it brought to the attention of the HR manager? As embarrassing as it may be for both parties involved (temporarily), it is much better to encourage a direct approach between employees within an organization than to have a whole department, plus others outside the department, involved.

Unfortunately, incidents of this nature occur day in and day out. In the incident cited, you have a perfect blend of gossip, rumor, and bullying complicated by triangulation all coming together.

Triangulation occurred with impunity, and the true culprits received immunity. What a waste of resources.

Accordingly, the behaviors associated with the various forms of conflict are *not* harmless. There is no such thing as harmless gossip. Never has someone been thankful for the untrue rumor being spread about them. Furthermore, working diligently on a project only to have someone else take all the credit for it, sabotaging your efforts, dedication, and hard work is never described as a warm and fuzzy feeling.

Negative conflict can be managed, however. The amount of time leadership spends dealing with these matters can be reduced. It takes commitment from leadership, education of employees, and consistency of application. It doesn't require more policies, more disciplinary action, and more fear being introduced in the workplace. Most importantly, leadership must understand the mission of reducing conflict and not contribute to this by adding fuel to a smoldering fire.

Leadership Fueling Conflict

To believe employees are the sole source of conflict within organizations would be a canard. There are bosses who, if not identified and dealt with, will continue to be the source of pain for their employees.

A bullying behavior found in schoolyards and among employees can also be found among leaders. Some leaders embrace a type of behavior which is designed to intimidate and demand compliance of people. This is just another form of bullying. What this does to an organization's climate can and will undermine any efforts made to curtail employee conflict. This demands that leadership's behavior be assessed and appropriately challenged.

There is real fallout when a senior leader uses an intimidation technique to guide their team. It creates a trickle-down effect. One cannot expect the downward flow of communication to be anything more or less than what was received from above. When leadership communicates in a dogmatic manner and with an iron fist of authority, a vicious cycle of stress is the corresponding result. The same type of stressful message will be delivered to the next level and the next until fear pervades the organization.

When leaders practice bullying, rarely do they take into account what a person may already have in terms of commitments to deliver. There is no guidance in terms of priority. This results in unrealistic expectations, a stressful environment, continued disengagement, and quite possibly, a decrease in customer satisfaction.

Thus, bullying can be considered another form of control.

Unhealthy Control

It was once thought that a leader who wasn't "in control" was a weak one. Accordingly, when they ascended to the top of the corporate food chain, they used control as leverage to keep power. The thinking was a person who loses control (power) then loses authority. This, unfortunately, became ingrained in management and leadership DNA.

The following chart compares how control was considered a part of the management wheel that was taught to previous generations of leaders. Conversely, new thinking on this sort of process does not employ the term control. It is one more way to lessen the reliance on control as a leadership device and one more way to prevent it from becoming an overriding reason for conflict.

Evolved Management

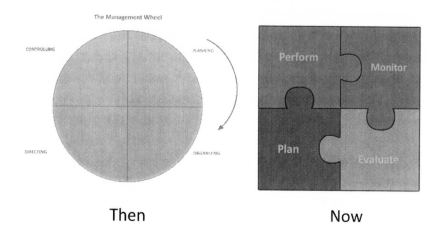

Then   Now

Being in control provides leadership a sense of security. The employee who uses a form of control, such as gossip or rumors, adopts a feeling of superiority. This is akin to a caveman beating up on another caveman to keep their tribe. For the employee, instead of fists, cruel whispers and petty remarks become the weapon of choice. For the leader, it is simply the use of control which is found in the adopted practices utilized for generations.

A conflict-free environment begins at the top. A poorly designed and communicated message can only have poor outcomes. They simply don't translate well.

Facts about Conflict

No organization is free of conflict. Too often, however, conflict is viewed with a level of acceptance by all employees, be it in small, medium, or large enterprises. However, if you are able to envision a day without conflict, a smile is sure to come across your face. This alone should send leaders searching for the magic potion to rid the day of conflict. Unfortunately, though, conflict continues to be alive and well even within the best-run organizations.

Even though conflict occurs everywhere, there is no reason for it to be a permanent resident or even acceptable as a cost of doing business. Some sources of conflict are noble and provide a pathway aimed at doing the right thing. It is the *negative* conflict that creates irritation, fear, and disengagement by employees, irrespective of where it occurs in the organizational structure.

Consider the cost of conflict. Here are a few numerically driven negative effects which damage the workplace. These types of behaviors should not be welcome in an organization striving to be its best. Moreover, they not only affect relationships, they cost time and create negative energy. They are also an additional and often unrecognized, unaccounted form of waste. Statistically,

- Conflict in the workplace causes up to a 20 percent loss to the bottom line regardless of organization size.
- Conflict causes turnover. This may result in a good employee *firing* their employer and finding an organization that is a better match for their values. This is an expensive result of mismanaged conflict. Turnover cost ranges 30 percent up to 150 percent of a person's annual salary. This causes a significant loss to the organization. For executives, this number is upward of 200 percent of the annual salary and bonus. In addition, the churn not only affects the loss of the individual but also costs related to things such as poor workplace relations. In other words, if conflict drives one's departure, this sort of turnover has far-reaching consequences for the organization.
- It has been reported that at least 20 percent of a typical manager's time is spent in dealing with conflict. This

includes putting out fires, addressing accusations and complaints, and doing other culture-robbing issues.

And the list goes on, including how conflict affects an individual's well-being and mental health either as a direct victim of conflict or as a bystander.

As mentioned, it is unlikely all conflict can be eliminated. However, there is a more efficient and effective way to reduce the amount of money lost and time spent dealing with destructive forms of communication. There are over one hundred degree programs in conflict resolution at universities and colleges across the United States compared to just a handful in 1980. This proves that people are not happy with conflict being an accepted, natural part of the workplace. Furthermore, conflict coaching is one of the fastest growing professions in the United States today.

Reaping the Rewards

The overarching theme of this chapter is to illustrate that negative conflicts, as described throughout, are not healthy for business, regardless of the type of business. Conflicts of this nature affect the bottom line and create an adverse effect on everyone involved.

Ultimately, negating conflict begins with sound communication and education of people. Senior leadership needs to communicate well—to all employees and other stakeholders—the behaviors which will be acceptable and what path to follow when observing those which are not in line with the values of the organization.

This communication needs to be clear *and* consistent. The message must include the reason behind the importance of acceptable communication, and leadership must be open to all questions or concerns over the processes being adopted.

So what exactly is this new process? What could possibly be so impactful to put a dent in the conflict which is seen every day and which takes up so much of our business day?

When employees are able to identify sources of conflicts, taught how to manage those who employ triangulation and with their efforts supported by proper leadership, the process of derailing conflict begins. By removing the vehicles which promote bullying, rumors, and gossip, conflict falls flat. We witness the birth of an environment filled with more positive than negative conflict. For instance, if you were to pass on gossip to a coworker who looked at you and said, "This is unacceptable according to the values of our organization and I will not listen any further," where do you think that story will go? Nowhere! It's that simple.

Organizations can simply spell out its values when addressing abuses. The culture normally and customarily takes care of these issues, providing the culture is a sound one. This is done by instilling the type of trust and commitment which breeds acceptance and inclusion rather than one which breeds contempt.

Today bullying combined with social media is found everywhere. There are numerous stories and reports of how social media is used to bully people, even to the point of taking their own life. These fill newspapers, media blogs, and the Internet, and even the federal government views some forms of this to be a hate crime.

To preclude unfortunate and unnecessary conflict requires a bit of education combined with coaching techniques. A person with bully tendencies is rarely prepared for pushback because they usually prey on the weak. Rarely do they expect someone to resist. When organizations provide their employees with support, knowledge, and mechanisms to effectively deal with conflicts of this sort, a potentially bad problem is precluded. Failure to take proactive and preventative measures only creates yet another issue leadership finds itself dealing with.

However, addressing the issue of bullying and eliminating it does not necessarily create overnight change. Providing the proper resources to address it is a starting point.

There is an age-old axiom that we always get what we tolerate. If you, as a leader, continue to accept bullying behavior, you will continue to receive it and you will be forced, one way or another, to deal with it. It becomes more difficult once the problem leaves the organization and lands in court or with government intervention.

To illustrate an effective method of dealing with triangulation, consider the following story. It has a happy ending but not before some pain points are experienced.

The issue

A newly hired human resources manager was approached by the walk-in clinic supervisor with a very old and very common problem. Two individuals within her department were just not getting along. As a result, and over time, each individual brought in other employees to support their interests. Sides were chosen with each successive issue. In other words, there were warring camps. Of course, this created dissension and division within this very public department. Teamwork and collaboration were not on anyone's radar screen.

The latest incident caused total department disruption. An elderly patient, who was simply looking to get an important maintenance prescription refilled, became the centerpiece. Two bickering employees were so busy clashing with each other that they ignored a call from the old man. As a result, his prescription was not refilled. This caused him to be admitted to the emergency room that same evening.

This incident became one involving more than casual employee sniping. It became more than backstabbing. It created a serious, life-threatening issue which enveloped the entire department. The newly appointed human resources manager was called in and became outraged, but not over this one incident alone. The basis for being irate was due to the fact that these warring factions had been allowed to go unchecked with issues unresolved for over two years. It was time to take decisive action.

A New Direction Attempted

Of course, the supervisor wanted one of the employees written up. But which one would be disciplined? The supervisor didn't care which one, just someone would do. A clear message needed to be sent to all.

However, the human resources manager had other ideas and tendered a new solution. As he explained, this wasn't a simple matter of providing someone with a warning notice. This had been attempted before with no substantive results noticed. In reviewing the history, it appeared the disciplinary action was spotty and inconsistent over the two-year period. Discipline had only exacerbated the problem among the warring factions.

After hearing both sides and gathering evidence, the human resources manager suggested a different approach to permanently fixing this issue, and others which preceded this one. It was time to bring this absurdity to a halt.

Rather than simply writing each employee up and invoking discipline, the human resources manager brought the two parties into a conference room, along with their supervisor. As he proceeded, the line of questioning was directed in a different manner. The patient became the focus. Care of the patient became the centerpiece of the discussion. Protocols were reviewed including ones surrounding telephone prescription renewals.

He then asked both parties, "Why weren't the established protocols followed?" Immediately, the old behaviors surfaced (finger-pointing and blaming). Then it happened. With calmness, the proper question was posed. "Who is more important here: the person to blame or the patient who wound up in the emergency room?" Neither could answer the question initially, but then both agreed the patient was most important.

Dialogue occurred between the two employees. They were talking to each other and not about each other.

However, a word of caution is in order. The new behaviors do not occur overnight. There are no shortcuts. Leadership must make the investment to educate and provide tools for employees to change. Habits form by ignoring poor behaviors or by dealing with them from a punitive rather than constructive mind-set. Leadership must enunciate the proper tone and be willing to remain resilient.

Leadership must be a reflection of the behavior they are seeking.

Chapter 7

Profound Leadership for Any Age: Brace Yourself for Inevitable and Undeniable Resistance

> Everything that can be invented has been invented.
> —Attributed to Charles H. Duell

Most people have never heard of Charles H. Duell, but at one time, he was the commissioner of the United States Patent and Trademark Office, the federal agency responsible for issuing patents. The rumor was he made an attempt to disband the agency and the quotation above was attributed to him.

There are disputes on whether or not he actually uttered the words, but it creates a good starting point for resistance that is inevitable when thinking about change and improvement. Especially when it comes to improvement of leadership.

The following quotations are indeed factual. There are diametrically opposed views between one's perceptions and reality.

"A cookie store is a bad idea. Besides, the market research reports say America likes crispy cookies, not soft and chewy cookies like you make."	Response to Debbi Fields' idea of starting Mrs. Fields' Cookies.
"Drill for oil? You mean drill into the ground to try and find oil? You're crazy."	Drillers who Edwin L. Drake tried to enlist to his project to drill for oil in 1859.

"The concept is interesting and well-formed, but in order to earn better than a 'C,' the idea must be feasible."	A Yale University management professor in response to Fred Smith's paper proposing reliable overnight delivery service. (Smith went on to found Federal Express.)
"Who wants to hear actors talk?"	H. M. Warner, Warner Bros., 1927.
"We don't like their sound, and guitar music is on the way out."	Decca Recording Co. rejecting The Beatles, 1962.
"I think there is a world market for maybe five computers."	Thomas Watson, chairman of IBM, 1943.
"640K ought to be enough for anybody."	Bill Gates, 1981.
"This 'telephone' has too many shortcomings to be seriously considered as a means of communication. The device is inherently of no value to us."	Western Union internal memo, 1876.
"The wireless music box has no imaginable commercial value. Who would pay for a message sent to nobody in particular?"	David Sarnoff's associates in response to his urging for investment in the radio in the 1920s.

Of course, the quotations appear almost comical, especially when viewed in hindsight. On a larger scale, they indicate an almost willingness in each of us to put limitations on ideas. The perception involves people who are supposedly on the leading edge of change.

Many years ago, as the United States was trying to transform itself onto a more quality conscious path, there was a poster that depicted the formation of an idea. It went from a bright idea for something new and innovative to a fade to dark as a result of relentless rejections of the idea. It looked something like this.

I have an idea!

Almost immediately, it was followed by "But it won't work," "It costs too much," or even "Just playing devil's advocate, but ..."

Soon, the idea fades to black, resembling something like this:

These are typical things that happen when new ideas are being introduced or improvements made. New ideas are not necessarily folly. The effects of dismissing them rather than exploiting can open up opportunities for competition and render your organization a dinosaur. We need to listen and look into the feasibility with a visionary prism. Even these have a mind-set too.

So what are some of the effects that transpire when we engage new ideas? What are the impacts of change, and how do we work through change? In other words, how do we evolve?

There is much psychological research in this area concerning our inherent resistance to change. For various reasons, humans have resisted change, whether from horse and buggy to automobiles or internal combustion engine automobiles to electric cars.

Let's examine what causes people to battle transformation, even when it's in their best interests.

There are multiple reasons, beginning with why we need to change in the first place. Diversity, demographics, labor shortages, and other dynamics will not allow business as usual. So these are some of the most compelling reasons to look at many things through a different prism.

A standard reason for change usually begins with something not being "right." It could be a result of technology, crisis, external threats, mergers, and so forth. In other words, there has to be some reasoning behind the change effort. However, sometimes just changing the leadership at the top is enough to drive efforts.

How many organizations get a new CEO and he or she decides to do something different for the organization, but within their individual comfort zone? Regardless of the reason(s), change usually follows this typical formula.

$$D \times V \times F > R = \text{Change}$$

The following are explanations to this accepted principle.

D indicates the dissatisfaction of the current situation.

V is the vision of what needs to be and can be done with the change.

F includes the first steps, plans, and mechanisms to take to make the change.

R is the actual resistance to the change initiative(s) proposed.

As can be seen, the dissatisfaction, vision, and first steps have to be *greater* than the resistance for any meaningful change to occur. Levels of dissatisfaction, vision, and first steps have varying degrees of emphasis and are not necessarily equal. In the formula, they are multiplied against each other and parts may be higher or lower than other elements.

The point is in combination, they have to succeed any resistance to change and actually overcome it. Otherwise, the change initiative will fail. In fact, studies indicate that 70 percent of all of change efforts do not produce desired results.

This leads to looking at reasons for change failing. Could there be a correlation with respect to present employee dissatisfaction with engagement, whereby 70 percent of employees are not engaged?

Perhaps.

We know that employee disengagement stems from a variety of factors, from incorrect hiring to loss of confidence in senior leadership.

Let's examine a few of them, which are supported by facts.

Did you know 35 percent of employee turnover generally occurs in the first six months of employment? This could mean the employee was hastily hired, the organization did not provide a realistic preview of the job, or a skill set mismatch occurred.

We also believe there may be too much reliance on appraising rather than coaching people. This means feedback loops are not in alignment and coaching glossed over, or simply not done properly.

Currently, about 85 percent of US employees are dissatisfied with *personal and professional growth*. This is a key driver to dissatisfaction. Of course, it is recognized that organizations of today are flatter than before and there may be fewer promotional opportunities. Gallup indicates that roughly 50 percent of all employers provide tools and methods for growth. The demand for this obviously outstrips the supply. So people go to another place to find this success factor. Sadly, this spiral will likely play out in their next job too. Even today, as indicated in an earlier chapter, 62 percent of employees would like to change employers, even considering the current economy is less than stellar.

Mix this in with employees not *feeling valued or recognized*. Studies enumerate that six out of every ten employees feel they have been taken for granted. This is caused by a variety of reasons including the imbalance of work to personal life. There is no denying Generation X and Generation Y will want more of this than generations which preceded theirs. In fact, a full 60 percent of all employees would presently forgo pay in some form just to have more personal and family time.

Finally, dissatisfaction stems from *leadership* itself. Gallup repeatedly quantifies that organizations with higher employee to management trust outperform lower trusting organizations by over 180 percent. Even in the best of times, only around half of employees believe management is concerned with their personal welfare. This leads employees to generally feel the organization is poorly managed.

These dissatisfiers illustrate an extremely damaging report card on management. At present, only 40 percent of employees surveyed feel their own organization is well managed.

Finally, eight employees out of ten feel senior leadership helps themselves by walking on the backs of the people and exploit the organization for their own personal gain. Employees have taken note that the average US CEO earns significantly more than the average worker. Moreover, the spread has increased almost exponentially over the past forty years. Have things materially improved for the workers since that time? Data suggests otherwise.

All this information presents a daunting challenge to the CEO of any-sized organization. It is no wonder that 70 percent of change efforts *fail*. There are simply too many variables that spin out of control.

Change can be effective, though it takes a new type of leader as suggested in chapter 1.

It starts with an effective communication plan and continues with assuring the ten new leadership competencies remain in the forefront. We can't lead and manage using old techniques and old paradigms that don't fit the modern workforce.

Accordingly, as important as it is for the change concept to be formulated, the leader must assure communications are clear and understood going forward. If not, then resistance becomes the outcome. Many times, resistance is strongly registered by those who believe there is nothing wrong with current norms. The true leaders understand this and take steps to avoid communications breakdown.

There is also the element of fear—fear of the unknown. People generally will take action and advance their movements if they truly believe and feel the risks associated with doing nothing, remaining stagnant, are significantly greater than going forward. We have all felt the trauma associated with loss, and loss is a real possibility whenever change occurs. It does not have to be a loss of job. It can be loss of esteem, power, authority, or many other issues. However, transparency and clearer understanding of what lies ahead is a key to overcoming inherent fears. When uncertainty is allowed to enter the change initiative, fear is driven to greater heights.

For example, if you ask a person to drive a car down a busy thoroughfare blindfolded, more than likely, they will reject the offer. Blind faith in this is truly... blind faith. The leader is thus required to provide a sense of security for those tentative to the aspect of going to a place that is unknown to them. The organization's vision and need for a better-desired future state needs to be articulated and expounded on during uncertain periods.

An excellent strategy for dealing with fear and uncertainty relies on a healthy dose of communications. Communications do not necessarily paint a rosier picture. There is sometimes real trauma along the path of change, and this should be recognized. Remember we are adults, and as adults, we can handle things more easily if we at least understand the path. When fear and uncertainty are acknowledged upfront, with the understanding things may be different, but organizationally better, these two concerns are minimized.

Each of us has probably had to deal with loss of a loved one or family member. There is a process and usually contains five distinct stages of grief. These range from denial and bargaining up to acceptance. Most people generally follow a similar path when dealing with personal loss.

Change follows similar phases.

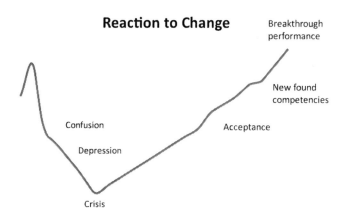

In the configurations above, one can easily see that once change is announced, it is often followed by denial, then anger and confusion, which leads to depression. It finally bottoms out in the crisis stage.

It is at this critical juncture leadership is needed the *most.* If the leader chalks up the venture as a losing proposition, then the effort fails.

However, when the leader encourages, inspires, communicates, and utilizes new competencies and tools, the tide turns. The new leadership proficiencies take hold and create a course for people to follow.

In other words, the leader keeps moving things forward. They keep swimming.

Paradigms

Part of the explanation for resistance may be found in the term *paradigms.* We all have them. Joel Barker explored this idea many years ago, and today, his observations are just as valid and just as predictable.

So what is a paradigm anyway?

In a basic sense, a paradigm is simply a model. Thomas Kuhn, an American historian and philosopher, explored the concept in a highly controversial book titled *The Structure of Scientific Revolution.* The book was published in 1962. It became very influential in both academic and ordinary circles. Kuhn wrote about a concept called paradigm shifts and the concept of paradigms and how they make us behave continues today. They help us see the importance of looking beyond myopic point of view and help us explore new pathways for seeking truth.

Kuhn explained the following:

1. Scientific fields of endeavor go through periodic shifts. They do not continue exclusively on a linear path or even in a continuous way.
2. These paradigm shifts allow new approaches to be seen and helps scientists discover understanding what they would have been unable to see previously.
3. Scientific truth, a noble notion, can never be determined by clear and objective means. This occurs only through a clear consensus embraced by the scientific community. These sometimes are impossible to measure or be compared because of competing realities that are difficult to reconcile. Accordingly, our understanding of science can never totally and absolutely rely on objectivity because subjectivity enters the picture. These biases must be accounted for.

Paradigms interfere with our ability to grasp new ideas. They cloud our vision, even to the point where we don't even recognize those things that are threatening us.

Here is an example of a paradigm from both sides.

There is a swirling global warming debate. Who is right and who is wrong? It's a matter of a person's point of view. Those who believe lowering earth's temperature by reducing carbon emissions are in direct odds with those who believe warming is cyclical in nature. In the 1970s, there was warning from the scientific community of an impending ice age. Now there is discussion and alarm over the possibility of entire cities being swamped as a result of melting polar ice caps.

When Kuhn published his book, he defined a scientific paradigm as "universally recognized scientific achievements that, for a time, provide model problems and solutions for a community of researchers." This meant

- *what* is to be observed and scrutinized
- the kind of *questions* that are supposed to be asked and probed for answers in relation to this subject
- *how* these questions are to be structured
- *how* the results of scientific investigations should be interpreted

To offer an explanation of this concept, let's look at the currently accepted paradigm of the standard model of physics. A scientific model allows for normal and customary investigations of various phenomena that may be contrary or even disprove the currently accepted model. However, funding through grants for research would be more difficult to obtain if deviations from the accepted model were too wide. In other words, certain models of physics have been accepted and to disprove the acceptance would establish a daunting task. An experimenter is more likely to receive funding associated with accepted principles than an experimenter who is trying to disprove an accepted theory.

This concept creates groupthink or its cousin: mind-set. It is more difficult to counter things that have been accepted. It's much easier to simply accept certain concepts as norms. Performance appraisal and incentives fall into this paradigm. This occurs in both small- and large-scale processes.

Accordingly, management and leadership fail to see the advantages of trying something different because they are hardened in their thoughts about why certain things won't or couldn't work. For example, many organizations continue the process of performance appraisal, thinking it is needed for communications or pay adjustments. Actually, the concept of performance appraisal is not the only tool for items those concerns. Yet they remain part of the corporate landscape and are very difficult to overcome.

Other organizations continue using a preset period of time formerly called the "probationary period." In the modern sense, what does this do to the new employee in terms of trust? How does it affect them as a member of a team?

In reality, this introductory period is an offshoot of the days when unionized shops offered no grievance protection for anyone within this specified time frame. The company did not have a contract with the employee, until they became a member of the bargaining unit. Therefore, all employees, labor and professional, regardless of being a member of a bargaining group, were placed into the ninety-day no-man's land. Not a member of the bargaining unit per se, and not a member of the organization ... yet. So when a simple issue such as this is addressed with leadership, what is often heard is, "Well, that is the one period of time we can make a judgment on someone without adverse consequences."

Really? Is this a mechanism that has outlived its usefulness? Yes. But it's been a hard sell to leadership. This is another example of how paradigms prevent us from doing the right thing for people. They prevent us from seeing the possibilities of the future.

The same thing could be said about corporate policies and procedures that appear almost adversarial in nature. Examine most any organization's death in immediate family policy and one can easily determine how the company views this unfortunate circumstance. Most are written with such rigidity that employees feel they must take full advantage of the policy. Imagine the complex meetings which occur whenever death in family falls outside the bounds of the policy, especially in the new diverse workforce of today and tomorrow. The definition of family is radically undergoing metamorphosis.

As leaders we are in a position to make changes that enhance rather than diminish relationships. Yet we fail to recognize this in so many ways.

We find ourselves making efforts to think outside the box, as any good management text encourage leaders to do. However, too often we spend most of our time inside the box. This corresponds with normal science that Kuhn found interesting. Kuhn's revolutionary science is when we clearly think outside of the box of predisposed notions.

A word of caution though. Revolutionary science as Kuhn discovered is usually unsuccessful, but when it is successful, it changes the entire view of science. When a shift occurs, it becomes the box in which we operate until proven obsolete.

Paradigm Shifts

In *The Structure of Scientific Revolutions*, Kuhn wrote, "Successive transition from one paradigm to another via revolution is the usual developmental pattern of mature science."

At the end of the nineteenth century, a statement generally attributed to physicist Lord Kelvin (the Kelvin scale and absolute zero) is this: "There is nothing new to be discovered in physics now. All that remains is more and more precise measurement." However, a scant five years later, a young patent clerk by the name of Albert Einstein published a paper on relativity. This challenged concepts laid down by Isaac Newton two hundred years earlier.

In this case, the new paradigm reduces the old one to a special case. While Newton's mechanical models are valid for approximation of speed, they *pale in comparison* to those associated with the relative speed of light, which Einstein claimed.

Philosophers and historians of science, including Kuhn himself, eventually accepted a modified version of the paradigm model, which blends his original view with the slow and steady model of change, which was the predecessor. Kuhn's ideas were revolutionary in its time. They caused a major change in the way that academia discussed science.

An argument can be made that it created a paradigm shift in history as well as the sociology of science. Perhaps, though, Kuhn himself could not recognize such a paradigm shift. Being a part of social sciences, people are able to continue to use earlier ideas to discuss the history of science.

Paradigm Paralysis

Perhaps the greatest barrier to a paradigm shift, in some cases, is the reality of paradigm paralysis. Paradigm paralysis is the inability or even refusal to see beyond the current models of thinking. Examples in history include Galileo's theory of planets orbiting around the sun, electrostatic photography (Xerox), and the quartz timepiece, which Joel Barker discusses in his paradigm films. All were rejected as nonsense at the time but became the new paradigm.

So in the modern sense, what are some of the paradigms of organizations that continue to exist today? Performance appraisal, rigid policies and procedures, and face time are all examples of today's paradigm paralysis. These are dominant even as the world changes before us. Telecommuting, distance learning, and employee autonomy are the new horizons that may impact commonly accepted paradigms of today.

Paradigms are shaped both by the community's cultural background and by the context of the historical moment. For instance, the widely held belief that performance appraisals are effective or incentives and bonuses create better results are two examples of dominant paradigms that currently exist. Yet on examination, are these beliefs really true?

There is ample evidence to disprove this, but they still remain an integral part of most organizations. In reality, performance appraisal is not a substitute for vigorous, robust conversations with employees. They are not substitutes for leaders to propagate this concept or for developing competencies of employees. However, many still believe in this particular paradigm and will challenge any notion which disputes these concepts.

We are on the fringe of the evolving nature of work and how it's performed. The following are conditions that facilitate a system of thought in order to become an accepted dominant paradigm. These are the mechanisms which allow the paradigm to shift and become the norms of tomorrow.

- professional organizations that give legitimacy to the paradigm
- dynamic leaders who introduce and purport the paradigm
- journalists and editors who write about the system of thought; they disseminate the information essential to the paradigm and give the paradigm legitimacy
- government agencies which give credence to the paradigm
- educators who spread the paradigm's ideas by teaching it to students
- conferences conducted that are devoted to discussing ideas central to the paradigm
- media coverage
- lay groups, or groups based around the concerns of lay persons, that embrace the beliefs central to the paradigm
- sources of funding to further research on the paradigm

Accordingly, we must constantly guard against allowing our individual paradigms which cloud judgment and block advances. We cannot afford to become complacent in uses of things that seemingly do not fit the future.

Here is an illustration of customer service. One is the old paradigm. The other is the new. You be the judge of effectiveness.

If you have ever had the pleasure (and this is not meant to be sarcastic) of having a problem with something purchased online at Amazon, it is a truly amazing venture. Amazon provides you with three ways to get help.

1. You may call and be placed in a queue for the next available customer service representative.
2. You can chat online to resolve it.
3. You can ask them to call you to avoid wait times.

This is where it gets amazing. If you choose option 3, no sooner than you click on this option and provide a callback number, your phone rings. On the end of the line is a friendly, helpful agent who anxiously waits to serve your customer needs. Their goal is to resolve your problem during this call. They are empowered to make the right decision, meaning they are provided the autonomy to handle the issue.

The experience itself is so remarkable that you become a loyal member of the Amazon family. You search their site before making purchases. Their prices along with the service and value create a lifelong relationship.

Contrast this to having to appear before any state DMV group. We are not casting aspersions but believe waiting in line, being treated as an object rather than a person, and waiting to hear the word *next* make for an unpleasant experience.

Most people, given the choice of handling things at the DMV versus a root canal, would opt for the root canal. The system is rigid, the counter help is unfriendly, and they are not given a great deal of latitude to resolve your problem. The bureaucracy takes hold, which is guided by the rulebook ... Next!

Do your employees have autonomy and flexibility to handle things, or are they placed into a bureaucratic system comparable to the DMV?

The choice is yours to make.

Joel Barker wrote, "Look at the fringe of things this is where you will find change." In today's world, and leadership in particular, the fringe is leading the way in change. There are things occurring in the world of business that will impact things in the very near term. These new ideas may lead the way for fundamental shifts in business thinking.

It's time to discover, develop, and deploy new thinking.

Chapter 8

Three-Dimensional Engagement: Discovery, Development, and Deployment

Education is not piling on information ... but rather
making visible what is hidden as a seed
—Thomas Moore

Discovery, Development, and Deployment

Part 1

The Beginning ... The Discovery Pillar.

For a very long time, management has relied on uneven methods for employee development. Management governed the process yet missed some marks. Additionally, employees were left out of the process. Their needs were overlooked. The result was total management control.

What helps in getting a handle on things begins with asking employees how they feel and what they want.

As a result of these mixed outcomes, we developed a system, an evolution of modern management. Our system encompasses three interrelated areas we call discovery, development, and deployment. This creates three pillars of the evolved workforce. It touches on those things previously shared throughout this book. This is evolution beyond the current and accepted state of things.

Let's create a visual which we can all relate to and easily imagine. It begins with an anxious group of middle school children who want to learn how to play a musical instrument. For many, their school is offering them their first opportunity to receive professional instruction to learn a new skill: to make beautiful, harmonious music.

As the children bustle about trying to decide which musical instrument they will be dedicated enough to lug back and forth to school each day, along with which will bring about the greatest amount of satisfaction, the process begins.

Students arrive with their instruments in tow for their first day of real instruction. They have great expectations for themselves and their fellow band members. They surely will sound like the bands they hear and see marching in parades, at athletic events, or in concert halls. Then it happens. Expectations meet reality.

The band director shows students important first steps in how to properly assemble their instruments, care for them, properly hold them, and get a sound out of them. How boring to the children. They simply wanted to start playing their instruments. And the director? Well, directors are accustomed to this reaction. They understand this is only the beginning. This is merely where the process starts.

The director gets a glimpse of the task ahead, while students have their immediate proficiency deflated. However, with the correct guidance, instruction, and coaching, all will be fine eventually.

And so the process of discovery for an organization begins. This is the point where leadership makes the commitment to embark on a journey. They are committed to finding a better way to engage their current employees and attract new talent. They want to build a group of employees who, together, make harmonious music.

However, before leadership can move forward, they need to understand where they are. Much like the band director learning things about her new class, the leader unveils things through their own assessment of the organizations. A thorough review of areas, such as communications, collaboration and teamwork, development, leadership, and systems, provides a starting point. This beginning may not be as bad as expected, or it could be worse than imagined. In either case, it creates a basis to build upon.

Very similar to the teacher who begins helping aspiring musicians become comfortable with their instruments, the leader has a clearer vision and understanding of where improvements need to be made. However, human nature compels us to jump in and begin fixing what has been found. We believe this is a time to pause and reflect. This is the moment where leadership is obligated to communicate to their employees a desired future state. Accordingly, this calls for vigilance and, more importantly, patience. It's time to reveal the plan.

A plan designed to create a culture where real employee engagement is realized becomes paramount. A clear and concise plan requires the leader to communicate with all involved the need to see the path ahead. Employees need to know what is in it for them and how critical steps will create a brighter future for everyone. Most crucially, employees need to know this is not another "flavor of the month" program. Employees must understand and believe there is a sincere approach to transformation, and leadership must communicate how they are responsible for seeing it through to fruition. Most employees have likely experienced numerous false starts as a result of hypocritical behavior from the past.

This is a vitally important step. Your actions must be *bold.*

Leaders who understand the importance of providing a clear path forward for their workforce will dedicate the time and energy necessary to prevent any mistaken interpretations along the way. Though it may seem trivial, the leader who insists on a better outcome will invest in this important step before the employee's journey begins.

As referred to in our chapter on mission, vision, and values, we know actions speak louder than words. Leadership must outwardly show their commitment to the organization, to the change for improvement, and to their employees. A leader's transparency encourages open communications and allows for challenges when actions do not reflect the message which is being communicated. For employees to view this commitment on a grand scale, opening a controversial topic up for discussion allows robust debate and feedback to transpire. Outward and bold action encourages meaningful dialogue to take place, possibly for the first time. This creates a noticeable signal of commitment and openness and must be part of the leader's new DNA makeup. After all, they aspire to create a new organization.

A crucial element of the discovery pillar requires leadership to embark on a path where inspiration rather than external motivators are instilled. Learning how to inspire begins with inviting open and honest feedback. For example, let's review the actions of Griffin Hospital in Derby, Connecticut, several years ago. This is an illustration of how open communications transform a troubled organization to one of engagement and one that was able to provide best practices for hundreds of hospitals across America.

Griffen's CEO, Patrick Charmel, began asking for honest feedback from employees, doctors, nurses, patients, and former patients. His style was simple. He committed to listening and then provided people with what they asked for. Today Griffin continues to be committed to transparency and open, honest communication between leadership and staff. Nothing is hidden, and there is constant communication of good *and* bad news. There is not a fabricated type of involvement from employees when major decisions are made. Employees' opinions and ideas are earnestly acted upon and leadership makes a point to solicit regular and timely feedback. Their routine includes publishing results of key decisions. It started with commitment to share information and has been followed up with consistent aligned behaviors of leadership.

Any organization that takes time to demonstrate sound leadership behaviors and commitments will receive greater and more honest feedback from employees. Conversely, any organization which does not follow this course runs the risk of spending a lot of time doing the same thing that has been tried before with minimal, if any, results.

Once a leader's resolve is discernible, the need for commitment and involvement from the employee is necessary. Akin to a teacher who explains the benefits received from a student's participation, a leader must provide a clear picture of an organization's future state. The desired outcome can only be obtained with employee involvement. This becomes the next building block in the discovery pillar.

When an environment of free exchange is established, employees will be excited to share their opinions. Leaders seek honesty from employees. This is an essential requirement for noteworthy results to be obtained. Whether data is received from an employee survey or individual sensing interviews, employees must feel free to express their thoughts. Both climate surveys and sensing interviews are simple, effective tools for gathering feedback from people.

More importantly, when employees understand leadership is thoughtful about creating a clear path to improve processes, systems, and work life, a strong and invaluable combination of honest feedback is created. The results can be revealing.

Unfortunately, many employees have been exposed to past surveys which resulted in little, if any, improvements. Therefore, surveys which are administered without a strong commitment to make things better will most likely create data that is not useful. Past baggage could inhibit poor employee buy-in.

But when people see actions behind words, there will be a renewed faith and employees will provide useful and meaningful opinions and subsequent data. Information obtained and communicated earnestly will remove any barriers and reluctance from employees, providing honest feedback in the future. This will eliminate a wall that many times inhibits an organization from moving forward. All stakeholders will have their voices heard.

Overall, sensing sessions and surveys create first steps in establishing a solid organizational baseline. The information obtained from these interrelated processes and used at the beginning of the discovery pillar is compared to information revealed in the organization assessment tool conducted with leadership.

The leadership assessment tool digs deep into key areas where management and leadership have tremendous impact. Notably, communications, collaboration, development, leadership, and systems owned by management are evaluated and measured for effectiveness. This helps identify where the gaps are and which ones need urgent attention. Designing a plan to address problem areas which affect both employees directly and the organization as a whole will have a tremendous impact on how employees embrace the rest of the journey.

However, discovering where an organization begins its journey is more than the use of assessments and surveys. Using these tools without a plan is like trying to teach a band class to read music without sheet music for them to see.

Leaders have a tremendous responsibility to provide an authentic foundation for the process to unfold. Accordingly, employees always take note of both what is being communicated to them as well as looking for consistent application of behaviors. The strategy will be carefully monitored by employees to see how leaders are adopting transparency. Generally, employees want to be included in the plan.

Employees expect a lot, but so do leaders.

Evolved leadership asks employees to embark on a profound journey of transformation together. This commitment will not be experienced with one isolated message or a single outward application of a new behavior. This evolution needs to happen multiple times for it to truly make a difference in the organization.

It needs to be witnessed, discussed, and sometimes challenged to assure the process creates what it was intended to do.

The goal of discovery is to set the stage whereby employees provide input and leaders take action. This allows employees to become excited about the path toward real employee engagement.

Part 2

The Development Pillar.

Whenever reviewing top reasons people leave their jobs, consistently found in multiple lists, and near the top, is lack of development. Isn't it best to find ways to maximize the talents of people you currently employ by offering them development opportunities?

As discussed throughout this book, whenever a person leaves an organization out of frustration or any reason, the result is unnecessary and waste. In today's world, employee churn simply costs too much for any organization to not find ways of maximizing the inherent desire most people have to achieve.

There are multiple common denominators which point to reasons why people leave their current jobs. The following are the most obvious ones.

Many times organizations unintentionally falsely misstate job content. Most people are anxious to begin their first day of their new job. After an exhausting vetting process, which may include multiple interviews, testing, job profiling, and reference auditing, the person arrives for the first day of the rest of their work life.

Imagine how they feel after they settle in a job which in no way matches what they were led to believe. It doesn't take long for the new hire to start thinking what other misconceptions are in store. The die is cast, and many times, there is no reset button that can be pushed.

Whether this is a result of rush to hire or the fact the new hire had a dynamic personality which overshadowed their given skill set, mismatches occur. This requires the candidate to meet the minimum expectations and qualifications along with the ability to integrate into the organization's culture. Knowledge, skills, and abilities (the KSAs) play a vital role in helping organizations avoid this pitfall. A dentist is ill equipped to perform neurosurgery and a neurosurgeon is not qualified to do dental implant surgery. A reason exists for base knowledge and should be followed, as much as a hiring manager feels the candidate could eventually fit into given situations. This is a disservice to both the candidate and the employer.

It's been proven money is not a motivator. However, it is a de-motivator when it's absent. Money normally affects the employer-employee relationship when there is perception of unfairness. Organizations must review their practices and have them in line with the local market. There is a lot of free information available on the Internet where employees can search and compare their pay with others within the same category and skill set. Employees will leave when these differences become too wide. Taking money off the table, meaning not allowing it to become a factor, is the best choice. This includes offering a benefits package that is also attractive.

In periods of transition, and especially with reduced headcounts based on economic factors, there are times where management requires a person to perform the jobs of two or more employees. While in the short term most people will step up and do this, in the long term, this is an invitation to burnout and leads to disengagement. When employees are forced to choose between a personal life and a career, oftentimes the employee chooses the personal one. The evolved workforce demands a better balance than previous generations.

People want recognition. Behaviorists have concluded this years ago. Most people relish praise and look forward to being lauded for a job well done. This becomes something of value to the person. The employer that does not do this can expect poor results in return. Organizations of all sizes must institute an effective way to communicate appreciation for efforts. After all, it's the human element that makes a difference in most situations and employment arenas.

One of the more common reasons employees leave (or fire their organization) boils down to lack of potential growth. Organizations are getting flatter, with fewer opportunities for upward mobility as viewed through previous generational prisms. Employers which find new, innovative ways to develop their employees and help them obtain new skills and even new responsibilities in current or future positions help pave the way for individual growth, which ultimately helps the employers grow.

Employees need to have some control over their work lives. This requires leadership to surrender and autonomy to be instilled. Whenever the manager micromanages all aspects of a person's work, the result is turnover. People are not lacking in their desire to have freedom in the pursuit of their given profession or skill. When employees are empowered and then given freedom to make decisions, they usually do the right thing.

Amazon is a perfect example of allowing this sort of freedom. People need latitude to resolve issues surrounding their employment. This creates trust and helps most organization's move forward.

Over time management has relied on the once a year or semiannual method of performance appraisal to sit with their employees and offer suggestions for improving performance. This is too little, too late. A large number of managers are clueless on how to earnestly help their employees improve. Moreover, many times, managers do not know how to give honest feedback, even though feedback is sought by their employees. A manager's role is steeped in helping people find the right mix. Unfortunately, the feedback often centers on telling them what to do but is devoid in helping them do it.

Many managers are promoted because they did their first job well, but that doesn't mean they know how to lead others. People skills can be learned and developed but it really helps if a manager has the natural ability to get along with people and tap into their intrinsic motivators. The modern manager or leader must understand both the nature of work and what makes people "tick."

People in general have trouble synthesizing the value of the typical CEO who makes obscenely more than the average worker. Added to this is the push to have people do more without a corresponding reason or fair value added. This is a perfect Petri dish of discontent. There is a common mismatch between seeing the correlation of revenues that are up as compared to competitive compensation. The employee wants a share but management is thinking of competition and the two don't mesh. Suspicion is thus created. Moreover, when the leader fails to walk the talk, this becomes fertile grounds for discontentment and disenfranchisement.

As outlined in an earlier chapter, data suggests the cost of turnover to be at least 30 percent of the employee's salary. It is much higher if the employee is an executive. As we all know, however, this is not just a financial matter for the person who leaves, or the company which is left. It is a matter of softer costs, such as the impact on morale, and hard costs, such as productivity.

Unfortunately, too many organizations fail to pay attention to the high cost of turnover, high costs associated with allowing turmoil to exist, and simply rationalize that when people quit, it's for the best of all concerned. Leadership needs to understand why people quit and, as noted, often it's due to one or more of the interrelated reasons found above.

If we were to look at this systemically, we would find the common paths each of these take. There are multiple interrelationships associated with loss of employees. The shadow of leadership is found everywhere.

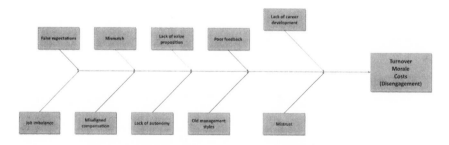

If leadership doesn't own this, who does?

A few years ago, we came across a situation where the head of HR was given a quarterly goal of reducing turnover. The HR professional owned only the part of the process that found qualified candidates who they onboarded into the system. The CEO, who established the employee's target, was apparently confused. He failed to understand the relationship between what indicators and practices the organization utilized that had both a direct and indirect bearing on turnover.

However, if an organization wants to really stop this madness, it must recognize culpability of actions and set in motion a plan and mechanisms to keep employees from leaving. A big part of this change is to outline a simple yet effective manner of employee development.

Individual employees are too often viewed as an afterthought, especially pertaining to typical performance appraisal plans and programs. Managers in many industries find that by the time they have gone through the intensive and time-consuming performance review process, they barely have enough time or energy to devote to an employee's development plan.

Accordingly, in many organizations throughout the world, employee-development plans are neglected, not completed properly, or poorly executed, thereby creating an ineffectual system of enhancing employee performance. Career planning and personal development grinds to a halt.

This does not have to happen.

When used correctly, employee-development plans should serve as a catalyst within the performance management process by building a structured pathway through which an employee can develop skills and address weaknesses identified in the total process. This begins as far back as the hiring process and includes the promotion process. Many organizations make a concerted effort to find the potential employee who matches all technical factors rather than capitalizing on one who possesses most of them. More emphasis could be placed on social skills, meaning the ability to adapt to the culture and more willingly developed. However, these people are often overlooked.

When an organization takes factors such as these into consideration, this creates an alignment that may enable employees to develop into high-performing individuals, enhancing their skill, and aiding the organization in its pursuit of business initiatives. Additionally, if handled properly, employees may be enabled to identify and acquire the skills they need to progress up the career ladder. This will become a necessity as skill shortages increase.

One particular recent study indicated that lack of career advancement opportunities was the *chief* and *most common reason* for people leaving the organization. To inspire, engage, and develop excellent performance, organizations must engage in solid career development. This is formed and becomes the basis of a properly designed and executed employee-development plan.

In addition, instituting individual development plans may even lead to the abandonment of typical employee performance appraisal. After all, why sit in judgment when the performance can be managed through more effective means? This is performance management and not performance appraisal. This helps guide a part of a system that drives so many interrelated areas and processes. This becomes a value-added proposition to the organization.

This is leadership evolving to suit work dynamics.

However, we must be cognizant of the fact that not all people learn or even develop at the same speed, or even in the same way.

Learning

There are basically three ways in which we learn. This is many times overlooked whenever something new is attempted. Adult learning requires a broader approach and multiple levels of techniques to assist in the learning process. Learners in general may fall into one of three categories.

1. **Visual.** This is a learning style in which ideas, concepts, data, and other information are associated with images and techniques and remembered through actual reading and absorption of words and symbols.
2. **Auditory.** Auditory learning styles encompass a manner in which a person learns through listening. Of course, an auditory learner depends on hearing and speaking as a main way of learning. They must be able to hear what is being said in order to understand and may have difficulty with instructions that are written.
3. **Kinesthetic.** This is a learning style where learning takes place by carrying out a physical activity rather than listening to a lecture or watching a demonstration. Kinesthetic learners rely on actually doing something in the learning process for the information to take hold and advance the skill.

With each style of learning, there are key characteristics that impact the way they learn. For example, a visual learner often is very good at spelling yet may forget a person's name after introductions. Additionally, they may need quiet time.

The visual learner also may have to think for a bit before understanding things that are unveiled during a spoken lecture and they often dream in color. Of course, this learning style appreciates things that are illustrated in charts and graphs, which creates a better understanding of data and information.

The auditory learner, on the other hand, is almost diametrically opposite in their approach to learning. This type of learner likes things expressed orally, such as reports. They also have a penchant for explanation of data and are natural at speaking out in group settings.

Because of their tendency to be better at speaking, they may read slower but follow spoken directions very well. Auditory learners also fit well in study groups based on the often used verbal exchanges that occur in these settings.

The kinesthetic learner is the type that learns by actually doing tasks, and their learning style encompasses a different blend of characteristics.

Oftentimes, they are good at sports. The kinesthetic learner cannot sit still for extended stretches of time. They usually are not too gifted as spelling but lean toward scientific laboratory settings. They are inclined and gravitate to movies and books which incorporate action and adventure. The kinesthetic learner also enjoys participating in role-playing exercises and has difficulty and may often fidget in a lecture-formatted way of learning.

Adult learners also possess at least four different learning styles. These are distinct and encompass different methods. An individual may be dynamic, imaginative, analytical, or common-sense learner. The following chart defines the distinctions in these learning styles.

Dynamic Learners	These are learners who are active, involved, dislike routine, and learn by trial and error or self-discovery.
Imaginative Learners	Learners who are imaginative learn by listening and sharing, seeking meaning, and require personal involvement.
Analytical Learners	These learners who are deliberate, unhurried, seek facts and learn by thinking through ideas and concepts.
Common Sense Learners	Learners who are efficiency oriented. They need to know how things work and learn by testing theories in logical and sensible ways.

The manner in which we are taught radically changes as we age and become adults. In the learning cycle as youngsters, there is little control over what is to be learned and how it will be learned. Accordingly, much time is spent in games (as adolescents) than lecture (as young adults.)

However, once we reach adulthood and develop our own experiences, the way we learn and what we accept is challenged. The experiences we have as children help shape learning, but as adults, we use different experiences to synthesize concepts.

Therefore, control which dominates the child's learning may have an opposite effect as we mature and grow in adulthood. Control over learning with children is generally accepted but radically changes as children enter adulthood. Decisions on what is to be learned and even how it occurs dramatically shift with age, as indicated in the following chart.

Differences between Children and Adults as Learners	
Children	Adults
Rely on others to decide what is important to be learned.	Decide for themselves what is important to be learned.
Accept the information presented at face value.	Need to verify the information based on their beliefs and experiences.
Expect what they are learning to be useful in their long-term future.	Expect what they are learning to be immediately useful.
Have little or no experience upon which to draw; have relatively "clean slates."	Have much experience on which to draw and may have fixed viewpoints.
Have little ability to serve as a knowledgeable resource to teacher or even fellow classmates.	Have significant ability to serve as resource to the trainer and fellow learners.

Learning Styles

The information listed below details the four learning styles found in adults. This helps explain that more than one style of instruction may be necessary for diversified employee groups in order to help them achieve specified learning objectives.

Type of learner	What appeals to them	What they dislike	Personal characteristics	When they train others
Dynamic	new things inquiry learning cooperation and group work trainer passive/ students active action and accomplishment	objective tests seatwork following directions doing research writing formality theory sterile environments	enthusiastic dynamic comfortable with others good starter jumps right in impulsive creative	like experiential learning include variety and drama use learner's expertise don't consider learners to be empty vessels like creative assignments and projects teach life and extol courage like student discovery

Type of learner	What appeals to them	What they dislike	Personal characteristics	When they train others
Imaginative	effective classrooms being personally involved harmony in the classroom	debates memorizing lectures being rushed rote learning textbook learning	perceive information concretely process reflectively believe in their own experience	ask how it will help students are sensitive to students' backgrounds believe knowledge should increase

	cooperative endeavors group work inquiry and insight	being singled out sterile environments insensitivity broad coverage vs. depth	team oriented good listeners think alone first then with a group caring of others in the classroom	personal insights like to work with students individually and in groups use cooperative groups and discussion believe in individual growth encourage authenticity

Type of learner	What appeals to them	What they dislike	Personal characteristics	When they train others
Analytical	time lines task orientation learning/ studying dissecting research routine repetition drills	creative projects role plays small talk warm-up activities discussion unclear deadlines impracticality irrelevance group work	organized follow a plan work independently precise, thorough, careful follow directions calculate the probabilities	believe in research are content experts like direct instruction manage by knowing facts encourage exceptional stuff

Type of learner	What appeals to them	What they dislike	Personal characteristics	When they train others
Common sense	getting to the point strategic thinking practical applications	fuzzy ideas theory and philosophy lecture impracticality group work	decisive hard workers problem solvers seek utility	like productivity and competence want to give students specific skills like to see

	plans and time lines justice trainer passive/ students active	unclear deadlines	and results take action on tasks like to be in control of the situation perceive information abstractly and process it actively	students use skills to become independent tend to be self-contained and focused use work stations coach and facilitate

The explanation of different learning styles helps explain why sometimes, no matter how hard we try, some people just don't "get it." Understanding the differences will help you as a leader identify and improve both large and small group training and learning scenarios. Better yet, it helps you understand your employees.

The following information also serves as a mechanism for translating theory into actual practice.

Translating Theory into Practice		
Theory	**into**	**Practice**
Adults remember *10 percent* of what they hear, *65 percent* of what they hear and see, and *80 percent* of what they hear, see, and do.	→	To increase retention, provide both auditory and visual stimulation and allow for practice.
The greater the degree of job relevance to the individual, the greater is the degree of learning.	→	Provide examples that are directly job related; allow practice in job like conditions.

Adults need to be able to integrate new ideas into what they already know if they are going to be able to retain the information.	→	Capitalize on the experiences of the audience to build new concepts; structure lessons to move from the known to the unknown.
Adults prefer self-directed and self-paced instruction to group learning led by an instructor.	→	If the training is done in a group led by the instructor, build in independent activities; consider trainee-focused approaches to training.
Adults bring a great deal of experience to training.	→	Capitalize on the experiences by facilitating discussions.
Integration of new knowledge and skills on the job requires application on the job.	→	Build in follow-up activities or action plans to be used on the job.

Having a solid grasp on how adults learn, their styles, and manner in which they learn are very important factors when instituting an employee-development plan which is vital to the development pillar.

Employee Development in General

A proper employee-development plan lays the foundation for individual and corporate growth. Elements of a good plan include the following:

- assesses and determines an employee's development needs
- actions taken to address the needs, such as internal and external training

- when the training will be done
- the support the company must provide
- actions the individual employee must take

To get started, let's review a system of employee development we believe in. Each part will be delved into further and greater detail provided. However, for starters, a recommended and proven development system resembles the following model.

THE EMPLOYEE DEVELOPMENT SYSTEM

1 Compensation Planning
a min--midpoint--max scale
80%   100%   120%

4 Employee Development
Manager/supervisor creates individualize plan
(1) Internal training
(2) External training
(3) Special work projects

Periodic reviews

This requires an additional step in the process.

2 Competencies
5 Core Competencies + KSA's

1. Intellectual
2. Interpersonal
3. Leadership
4. Organization
5. Self Management

5 The Annual Review

Should be no surprises
Not judgmental
Two measures:
(1) Development need
(2) Performance strength

Measures these

3 Uniform Job Descriptions based on KSA and Competencies

6 Cycle repeats

These create value for both the company and employee

The first thing an organization needs to do in terms of establishing a development process is to recognize the role money plays into the development. As we have discussed in several places in previous chapters, the typical appraisal process incorporates a money aspect. We believe money should be taken off the table at the outset. When this element is removed, the focus becomes clearer. However, we believe organizations must perform compensation planning and establish a philosophy such as market pay that is easy to administer. After this is properly determined, then leave money off the table and pay according to the plan.

Secondly, we believe organizations should spend time understanding their own core competencies and develop competencies that are in alignment with the organizations core ones. Many times organizations do an excellent job of developing knowledge, skill, and abilities of individuals, but the process stops there. The KSA typically does not drive the organizations forward. Competent employees do.

As we head deeper into this century, we feel there will be greater emphasis on developing the worker. They will become more and more knowledge-centric as technology becomes more pervasive in society. The charge for organizations is to develop competencies that are properly and fully aligned, which enable employees to enhance organizational effectiveness.

A typical knowledge worker would thus have a set of universal competencies. Moreover, for the knowledge worker these will most likely entail the following ones:

- intellectual
- interpersonal
- leadership
- organization
- self-management

You will note that leadership is listed as a knowledge worker competency. There are valid reasons for this. We envision organizations continuing to flatten in this century. More people may become permanent part time and many will be considered contingency workers (such as consultants) who arrive to help with special projects but are not permanent to the organization.

Flatter organizations will require more work being performed in a team setting as work becomes more project focused. Team-centered work requires shared leadership to be effective. Of course, the natural work team will continue to have the element of a decision maker (such as department head), but the real work more than likely will be centered on projects. Accordingly, shared leadership as outlined in a previous chapter becomes the norms for teamwork.

However, the leadership competency may have multiple definitions that support it. For example, in our model, leadership is further defined as being

1. Visionary
2. Change management
3. Leadership
4. Delegation
5. Managing people
6. Managing quality

It is likely the knowledge worker will find themselves in situations, and on a regular basis that requires these competencies to be employed. These competency definitions then become a key element of employee development.

The third component of the employee-development process is the proper design of uniform job descriptions. Job descriptions are helpful to both the new and the established employee to understand what is necessary to them as well as the organization.

However, many times, job descriptions are poorly done. The analysis of the job is missing and the document becomes merely a set of duties that must be performed. These sorts of descriptions guide the tasks but do not guide or reinforce the development. A sound analysis of the job, which provides a clear path for company growth and individual development, should be undertaken. A well-written job description encompasses knowledge, skills, and abilities but should also contain the associated competencies necessary for success.

After the compensation strategy is set, competencies established which are reinforced through properly designed job descriptions, the next phase of employee development centers on the actual development plan.

The development plan does not need to be elaborate, but it certainly needs to be done. We favor a process whereby the leader (regardless of whether they are a supervisor or manager) visits with the employee to establish a meaningful plan. This plan should incorporate elements of

- internal training
- external training
- special projects

As mentioned earlier, projects are likely to greatly influence the organization of the future and they become teachable moments. The training plan that incorporates three development areas as outlined above helps identify the competencies that are necessary for upward organizational mobility; individual, personal growth; and growth for the organization.

The competencies then become easily measured. This is the final step in the development process.

For generations, leaders have been reliant on assessing performance through typical appraisal processes. During this time, however, employees have come to disdain the approach while management feels forced into sitting with employees on some basis (usually at least annually) and retrace past performance of the individual. We believe there is a better way.

If the leader or the organization believes there must be some "mechanism" which paves the way for assessing "performance," we suggest an alternate route to this.

Rather than focus on behaviors such as attendance, reliability, quantity, and quality of work, why not try something radically different? Employ a different slant on this by providing an opportunity to review outcomes of the training plan.

This is easily accomplished through a performance management tool. This tool is once again easy to administer and provides real feedback to the employee and measures the attainment of competencies, rather than behaviors. However, the measures themselves are simple.

Rather than evaluating an employee's performance based on "Poor—Fair—Good—Excellent," which is typically found in a performance appraisal, why not focus on two outcomes? Did you do well or did something happen? However, it should be noted that neither outcome is solely tied to the employee. Many times, the current system inhibits their ability. But we have focused for so long on blame, rather than improvement, people have become the culprits.

A performance-management assessment tool eliminates this because the focus is on development *and* improvement. We think it's more difficult to assess things on a graphic rating scale than to have a conversation with the employee to determine next steps. Typical appraisals create an aura of judgment whereas the performance assessment creates a system of inspired, breakthrough performance.

We may even one day recognize there is no longer a need to judge an employee's performance, because they will be performing at levels unseen before. That is engagement.

This leads us to the next step in our journey: deployment.

Part 3

The Deployment Pillar.

The young band continues to practice. The band director who first discovered a group of anxious youngsters has systematically developed them into budding musicians. What began as fingernails on a chalkboard now resemble a collection of blended, diverse talent. They are now making music. There is one more step though.

They will showcase their hard work at the annual spring concert. How can we incorporate this chain of events into our organizations?

In the discovery phase, you *assess.* This means you employ surveys, interviews, and organizational assessment tools to determine a new path. Using this information, you are now armed with a clear picture. The organization begins to find itself. This is the foundation, a starting point, and reveals areas either needing a lot or little improvement. This first step is as important as any in the discovery, development, and deployment process. It is the point where commitment is pledged, the process is communicated, and a clear and concise direction is established. However, if this step is done in isolation, it leaves employees hanging and contributes to false starts. In fact, seven out of ten employers which collect data of this sort do not move to the next step and use it as a transformational mechanism.

If you are in one of those 30 percent of organizations that *are* paying attention, you are equipped to bring your organization to the next essential level. This is a move from discovery into development and requires a strong commitment to all stakeholders. If done correctly, all people throughout the organization will better understand their purpose, feel valued, and embrace the continued development needed to drive things forward today and well into the future. A vibrant, meaningful pathway is created.

To illustrate this point, we continuously poll various groups, organizations, and other thought leaders. Our polls consistently reflect and clearly reinforce perceptions related to employee engagement. For example, when asked to name the predominant factors associated with disengagement, the following results are the common themes we find.

Factors	Percentage
Mismatch of behaviors to stated values	45
Management by numbers	18
Lack of employee development	18
Unclear strategic plan	14
Lack of autonomy	5

Employees want to be engaged. The discovery and development phases address and intertwine issues which matter most to today's workforce. They set the tone as well as outline desired new behaviors.

It is not until all of these pieces are in place, and more importantly systematically embraced, that it is time to deploy, time for the spring concert. This is where we find understanding within the system. After an organization successfully moves through discovery and development, it is time to deploy the stakeholders. Employees begin to understand that commitment is more than picnics, ice cream socials, or free soda. These perks have been inappropriately labeled as engagement enhancers. Whatever on the surface success they have enjoyed, they have deluded our way of thinking about this subject. Many times, feel-good initiatives such as these have arrested real employee engagement. This is foofaraw as Dr. Scholtes explained.

But when an organization improves this particular element, it becomes a worthwhile investment and not an expense of doing business. It is the business. Rather than attempting to prove the worth in financial terms, it clearly impacts the organization's bottom line. It is improvement in financial performance.

Consider the following attributes.

According to a recent post by the *Wall Street Journal* and the iOpener Institute, this is what you can expect from a population of employees who are involved. Employees

- stay twice as long in their jobs
- believe they are developing their potential twice as much
- spend 65 percent more time feeling energized
- are 58 percent more likely to go out of the way to help their colleagues
- identify 98 percent more strongly with the values of their organization
- are 86 percent more likely to recommend their organization to a friend.

All in all, these are desirable traits, especially in a critical labor shortage era.

Clearly, a well-designed plan sounds picture perfect on paper. We understand, though, that progress has a way of attracting naysayers. There will be moments when all of it seems to be too much of an undertaking and a leader is faced with the dilemma of forging ahead or standing pat. Static is not an option, and if chosen as the path, it will likely result in an organization experiencing another false start—or worse, ceasing to exist. Resilient leadership knows what needs to be done at this juncture. This is the point where buoyant leadership is needed most. Leadership is difficult at times. However, if properly focused and able to reflect on the organization's original state and visualize the result, they will pull through the transformation and come out much better than before.

Therefore, a leader must remain cognizant that with each step, every day and with each piece of communication, consistency must be present. This consistency in word and deed is crucial and must directly reflect the organization's stated mission, vision, and values. Failure to do so will result in the journey denigrating into yet another flavor of the month.

Until this new philosophy and course of action becomes ingrained, we feel it is important to check decisions made against the organizations mission, vision, and values. This will help explain why a specific decision is made and allow the organization to find clarity in their actions and project the image they are striving for.

Finally, this process must be revisited in its entirety and continuously improved. As we know, each year produces another spring concert. An organization must resist complacency. This requires continued assessment, development, and deployment.

The result for a band director who discovers, develops, and deploys a group of musicians is the music. In terms of an organization which follows the same general process with their systems and employees, the results are *real employee engagement.*

We believe leaders who follow through with the steps outlined in this chapter will soon realize the importance of a system of engagement. Accordingly, they enhance their ability to help the organization remain competitive and vital in their industry. Moreover, they position the organization to attract new talent for continued and future success.

Employees who willingly adapt are more than just happy employees, although we realize this is better than a bunch of unhappy ones. The essence of discovery, development, and deployment results in employee engagement. It is leadership's duty to involve the workforce, especially when the goal is higher production, lower turnover, fewer errors, and less drama in the workplace.

When analyzing top, mid and bottom segments of a typical organization, we find that though the engagement is substantially higher for the manager, it continues to be lower than the level above them.

For example, senior leaders are currently 70 percent engaged, the level below this are 62 percent engaged, and typical employees are only 30 percent engaged. To incorporate breakthrough performance, all engagement levels will need to be improved, especially in the 30 percent level experienced over the previous thirteen years. Even though many efforts have been made to improve this important aspect of the business, few if any have produced tangible results. If these trends remain and are accepted, potential profits resulting from a vibrant workforce will continue to be untapped. Appropriately incorporating our process to improve will result in expansion at all levels.

The manager's role in engaging the workforce must not be underestimated. Not only do they have tremendous interaction with employees, they strongly influence the climate within their area of responsibility regardless of what occurs outside their jurisdiction. Typical manager engagement scores are better than that experienced by the US worker, but they are not necessarily totally engaged. As a result, it is important that a manager's involvement be recognized and factored into the equation of the organization one. It is essential that all levels of engagement be checked and addressed when this full cycle is adopted.

There is a strong correlation between leadership surrendering their control and employees gaining autonomy. Once this combination is achieved, the start of an inspired workforce is experienced. Organizations instituting a new way of thinking will also want to reconsider the practice of management by numbers alone. When basing decision on numbers only, organizations overlook financial numbers that are directly impacted by the human equation. Low engagement scores can be tied straight to a cost per employee and have been sadly ignored.

For example, organizations experience an average loss of $10,000 per employee in profit due to low participation and willingness. This is very significant because, in comparison, a thriving workforce is 78 percent more productive and 40 percent more profitable than a poorly engaged one. When fully understood, the impact employee engagement scores have on an organization's bottom line reveals a compelling reason for this initiative to be a priority in the minds of leaders and in a company's strategic plan.

Traditionally, and as illustrated throughout this book, we have had a tendency to assign blame on a variety of things whenever situations don't quite pan out. To do so in terms of low employee engagement won't solve this issue. It is not the newer generation of workers and it is not necessarily the economy. We believe it's something involving leadership. After all, they own most of the processes and systems found in typical organizations.

Evolved leadership holds the key to a better way of leading and managing the organization. The evolved leader needs to understand systems, motivation, teams, and learning and be willing to instill a new sense of responsibility and course of action into the organization.

Many years ago, in the midst of the quality revolution in the United States and the world, there was a phrase which summed it up best.

> *If you always do what you've always done, you will always get what you always got.*

It's time to change our DNA.

We close this chapter with an illustrative graphic. It helps understand how the three pillars of discovery, development, and deployment come together to form an engaged workforce.

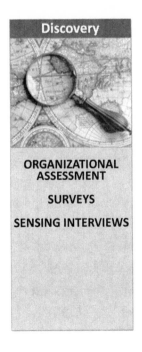

Discovery

ORGANIZATIONAL ASSESSMENT

SURVEYS

SENSING INTERVIEWS

Development

COMPETENCES:

- Knowledge workers
- Integrators

TRAINING PLANS

Internal
External
Special project

PERFORMANCE MANAGEMENT

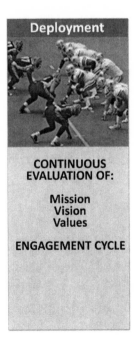

Deployment

CONTINUOUS EVALUATION OF:

Mission
Vision
Values

ENGAGEMENT CYCLE

This is a system that will yield long-term results.

Chapter 9

The Evolved Workforce: Makeup of a Modern Workforce and Workplace

Just when I think I have learned the way to live, life changes
—Hugh Prather

The second decade of the twenty-first century represents a puzzling set of situations. The future seems nebulous at times, and we seem to be faced with incongruent pathways and circumstances.

Here are some real anomalies and facts of today.

- Real unemployment in the United States stands at around 13 percent (U-6 data).
- The unemployment rate (meaning those receiving unemployment compensation) hovers at levels substantially higher than what is customarily accepted as full employment.

Yet

- Wall Street is experiencing record-breaking highs with the market up over 30 percent from ten years ago.
- There are skill shortages in key industries, especially among tradespeople.

And

- Demographics are continually shifting with more foreign-born workers being employed.

- The last of the baby boomers, born in 1964, reached age fifty in 2014.

Today, we are in a down economic cycle that the United States has experienced many times before. These cycles are cycles because they come and they go. We are indeed in the midst of some very confusing times. But old ways of leading people are not cyclical. The past leadership techniques and methods taught and utilized for generations of people will not work going forward.

Here is a case in point. In the wildly popular show *Dirty Jobs,* Mike Rowe works in less than attractive conditions, performing tasks that more than a few find demeaning. Why does he do this? We think it's to illustrate visually the opportunities that often go ignored in the United States. Mr. Rowe has stated in interviews, "We seem to be misleading younger workers and even pushing them into obtaining a college degree for jobs that don't exist or may not exist in the near future."

We have unintentionally, though nobly, encouraged all people to further education through obtaining a four-year degree, even though there are greater needs elsewhere. We also have placed an imaginary value of success that can only be realized by the college diploma. Today, we find ourselves facing critical skills shortages in the trades. Yet it is not uncommon for a qualified welder to be paid a six-figure salary. Even *Fortune* 100 petrochemical operations are experiencing difficulties in finding qualified operatives to maintain their facilities. Google is now placing less emphasis on the diploma and more emphasis on an individual's learning capacity.

However, society appears to value a Wall Street broker higher than the plumber who fixes your leaky pipes. Money is not a measure of success. The real measure of success is the value a person delivers. It is time to embrace a new way of thinking about *everything.*

The one thing leadership can do in the mind-set of all these uncertainties is ... lead.

Over the course of the previous eight chapters, we have laid out key concepts that will work regardless of cycles. If we engage our employees, make them a part of our total makeup, these seemingly confusing issues and times can be overcome.

But it takes leadership. It takes a willingness to look at the horizon with an eye for clarity, employee involvement, and many other things necessary for embracing the future. If leadership continues to focus on the past to deal with current problems, they will never be able to see what it will take to manage and lead now and well into the future.

We believe there will be a need to revamp many organizational aspects as we move deeper into this century. We have compiled a few which should be considered.

The pace of change will continue to accelerate and not slow down. This means the current climate will not be the same in five, ten, or twenty years. And we also know parochial interests will limit and impede the ability to move forward.

Here are a few notable organizational changes that are just over the horizon. We are not advocating *any* of them as the answer. However, they are gaining traction, and as leaders, we need to at least understand the makeup of them.

Mondragon Corporations

A few years ago, a close friend clued us in on the Mondragon organizational structure. We then found a robust Internet paper and discussion of this by Joel Barker, a leader in the field of study relating to paradigms. The following is adapted from this.

A Mondragon Corporation is a corporation and federation of worker cooperatives which originated in the Basque region of Spain. Founded in the town of Mondragon in 1956, its origin is linked to the activity of a modest technical college and a small workshop producing paraffin heaters.

Currently, it is the seventh largest Spanish company in terms of asset turnover and the leading business group in the Basque Country. At the end of 2010, it was providing employment for 83,859 people working in 256 companies in four areas of activity: finance, industry, retail, and knowledge.

The Mondragon co-operatives operate in accordance with a business model based on people and the sovereignty of labor, which has made it possible to develop highly participative companies rooted in solidarity, with a strong social dimension but without neglecting business excellence. The cooperatives are owned by their worker-members, and power is based on the principle of one person, one vote.

The ties that link the Mondragon cooperatives are strong. These bonds stem from a humanist concept of business, interrelated by a philosophy of participation and solidarity along with a shared business culture rooted in various concepts. These include basic principles, a shared mission, and the acceptance of a set of corporate values and general policies of a business nature.

Over the years, these links have been structured in a series of operating rules approved on a majority basis by the cooperative congress. The congress regulates the activity of the governing bodies of the corporation (standing committee, general council), the grassroots cooperatives, and the divisions they belong to, from the organizational, institutional, and economic points of view as well as in terms of assets.

This entire framework of business culture has been structured on the basis of a common culture derived from basic cooperative principles in which the Mondragon is deeply rooted. These include

- open admission
- democratic organization
- sovereignty of labor
- instrumental and subordinate nature of capital
- participatory management
- payment solidarity
- inter-cooperation
- social transformation
- universality and education

This inspirational philosophy is complemented by the establishment of four corporate values:

- cooperation, acting as owners and protagonists
- participation, which takes shape as a commitment to management
- social responsibility, by means of the distribution of wealth based on solidarity
- innovation, focusing on constant renewal in all areas

This business culture translates into compliance with a number of basic objectives (customer focus, development, innovation, profitability, people in cooperation, and involvement in the community) and general policies approved by the cooperative congress.

These are taken onboard at all the corporation's organizational levels and incorporated into the four-year strategic plans and the annual business plans of the individual cooperatives, the divisions, and the corporation as a whole.

A unique feature of the Mondragon structure is how it administers regulation of wages.

At a Mondragon, there are agreed-upon wage ratios between the worker-owners who do executive work and those who work in the field or factory and earn a minimum wage. These ratios range from 3:1 to 9:1 in different cooperatives and average 5:1. That is, the general manager of an average Mondragon cooperative earns no more than five times as much as the theoretical minimum wage paid in his or her cooperative.

This ratio is in reality smaller, because there are few Mondragon worker-owners that earn minimum wages, their jobs being somewhat specialized and classified at higher wage levels.

Although the ratio for each cooperative varies, *it is worker-owners* within that cooperative who decide through a democratic vote what these ratios should be. Thus, if a general manager of a cooperative has a ratio of 9:1, it is because its worker-owners decided it was a fair ratio to grant and maintain.

In general, wages at Mondragon's, as compared to similar jobs in local industries, are 30 percent or less at the management level and equivalent at the middle-management, technical, and professional levels. However, and as direct result, Mondragon worker-owners at the lower wage levels earn an average of 13 percent higher wages than workers in similar for-profit businesses. In addition, the ratios are further diminished because Spain uses a progressive tax rate, so those with higher wages pay higher taxes.

B Corporations

Another emerging organizational structure is the B corporation, which stands for "benefit." A benefit corporation is a class of corporation required by law to create general benefit for society as well as for shareholders. Benefit corporations must create a material positive impact on society and consider how their decisions affect their employees, community, and the environment. Moreover, they must publicly report on their social and environmental performances using established third-party standards.

The chartering of benefit corporations is an attempt to reclaim the original purpose for which corporations were chartered in early America. Then, states chartered corporations to achieve a specific public purpose, such as building bridges or roads. Their legitimacy stemmed from their delegated charter, although they could still earn profits while fulfilling it.

Over time, however, corporations came to be chartered without any public purpose, while their purpose degraded to one of being legally bound to the singular purpose of profit-maximization for its shareholders. Advocates of benefit corporations assert that this singular focus has resulted in a variety of societal ills. These include the spoiling of democracy, diminished social good, and negative environmental impacts.

Of particular note, in April 2010, Maryland became the first US state to pass benefit corporation legislation. This was followed by Hawaii, Virginia, California, Vermont, and New Jersey. In addition by November 2011, benefit corporation legislation had been introduced or partially passed in Colorado, North Carolina, Pennsylvania, and Michigan.

By 2012, eight states allowed benefit corporations legal standing. While there is some discrepancy of what states call a B Corp because the focus is on a changing concept of what a corporation should be doing for society.

Furthermore, a typical corporation may be formed for any legal purpose, and shareholders may set forth in its charter the purpose to serve general or specific public benefits or to take into account nonfinancial considerations. However, a standard corporation does not take advantage of this ability and is instead operated primarily for the financial benefit of its shareholders.

Even in such cases, "constituency statutes" permit directors and officers of ordinary corporations to take into account nonfinancial interests, such as social benefit, employee and supplier concerns, and environmental impact, but their general fiduciary duty is to *maximize value for the shareholders of the business.* In fact, shareholders would be able to bring civil claims against the directors or officers if they stray from their fiduciary duties to the owners of the business.

However, benefit corporations are not just permitted to look toward public purposes but must legally account for a variety of considerations as it pursues its mission. "Fiduciary duty" for benefit corporations must include nonfinancial interests, such as social benefit, employee, and supplier concerns, along with environmental impact.

A corporation, whether organized as a legal benefit corporation or as an ordinary corporation, can seek third-party certification on whether it fulfills this broader definition of fiduciary duty.

A benefit corporation thus resembles a C corporation or LLC, except for the requirements that its charter address these nonfinancial interests.

Low-Profit Limited Liability Corporations (L3C)

A low-profit limited liability company (L3C) is a legal form of business entity some states within the United States created to bridge the gap between nonprofit and for-profit investing by way of providing a structure that facilitates investments in socially beneficial for-profit ventures. The L3C simplifies compliance with Internal Revenue Service rules for "Program Related Investments."

L3C is a new classification of an organization. The organization uses its for-profit efficiencies along with fewer regulations from the IRS to achieve *socially beneficial* goals. An L3C is taxed as an organization that operates with a stated goal of achieving a social goal while making profit a secondary consideration and goal.

To authorize L3Cs, legislation must be lawfully passed to amend the General Limited Liability Company Act (LLC). So far, legislation has been approved in Illinois, Louisiana, Maine, Michigan, North Carolina, Rhode Island, Utah, Vermont, and Wyoming. Legislation has also passed in the federal jurisdictions of The Crow Indian Nation of Montana and The Oglala Sioux Tribe. Additionally, legislation has been written in California, Florida, Georgia, Iowa, Minnesota, Nebraska, Ohio, Texas, Washington, and Wisconsin.

As anyone can see, there are movements, some even supported by traditionally conservative states, to restrict avarice from infiltrating organizations. We have implied throughout how money alters organizations' ability to do the right thing. Whether its performance appraisal, where this is used to financially reward people, or incentive plans, humans react differently whenever money is used as a motivating factor.

There are many things changing from the reason for chartering new corporations to how corporations are structured. Moving into the future, we feel the typical hierarchal structure will be rendered obsolete.

What will the new organization look like? We can't be certain, but there are issues which are having an effect on corporate structure, pay, and so forth.

Just a very few years ago, a movement called Occupy Wall Street gained national attention as younger people made an attempt to illustrate the disparity between the top 1 percent of earners and the remaining 99 percent. The movement was radicalized a bit and the public grew disenchanted with the group's behavior and associated violence, which caused the movement to lose esteem. However, they did draw attention to the vast disparity that Mondragon's, B Corps, and L3C organizations avoid.

Presently, the CEO of a publicly traded company earns 207 times more than the average worker. The commissioner of the National Football League enjoys a thirty-million-dollar annual salary, even though it's legally structured as a nonprofit organization. Both sets of data seem peculiar as well as disengaging to the workforce.

In the United States, we have an emerging group of workers who do not equate money necessarily with success. A newer and evolving workforce places emphasis on social media, equality, and technology.

We also know public policy is being shaped by key events. There are legislators wishing to address and limit the income gaps between the highest paid people and the lowest paid. We also know public policy and law is now creating a different dynamic for organizations. For example, the Affordable Care Act and its implementation are currently forcing companies to take a hard look at classification of work hours.

According to the law, an organization with more than fifty employees must provide access to health care. Furthermore, the government has stipulated a full-time worker is anyone who works thirty hours a week.

This has many organizations

1) limiting their growth to keep employee headcount to under fifty people
2) keeping work hours below the thirty-hour mark where the organization has to provide access to health care.

Only time will tell the final outcome of this. However, a future organization may resemble the following graphic.

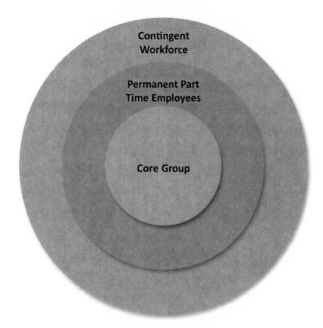

A Future Look

In this illustration, it is possible the organization of the future will resemble a concentric circle with roles filled as follows.

- a core employee group that is considered permanent to the organization.
- a permanent part-time workforce that works less than the traditional workweek, with limited benefits and perquisites.
- a contingent workforce composed of contract employees and consultants who work on projects, perform a service, and are never part of the permanent organization.

If this model holds true, it is even more incumbent on the modern leader to provide leadership to a diverse group. Leadership skill will require management of teams, sound communications, and constantly manage conflicting priorities, as well as support and cope with constant, ever-evolving change.

This won't be an easy journey, but it will be a fulfilling one. To embark on it, the modern leader must be willing to let go and be willing to surrender myths, rituals, and old DNA.

Chapter 10

Just Keep Swimming

Just keep swimming, swimming, swimming.
What do we do? We swim.
—Dory from *Finding Nemo*

Thoughts on New Leadership and Evolving the Workforce

We have been on a journey in this book.

You have been introduced to new ideas, discoveries, and some less than traditional thoughts. To wrap things up, we are leaving you with some beliefs on leadership and a few other items. We feel they make sense and are strongly supported by facts derived from a variety of resources. First, the following is a model of leadership that will work in any organization: public, private, or government.

Over the course of the previous chapters, you have been involved in understanding a new way of leading people and processes. Each chapter is interrelated and together provides a systemic way of achieving leadership success. Below is our model we developed over time and utilize when training within organizations. This is a model that will work in any age and at any time.

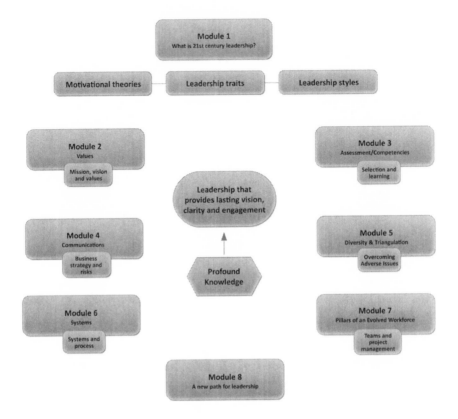

Our approach is unique.

We are now in a connected world which calls for a different brand of leadership. As mentioned in chapter 1, the evolved leader is required to have a set of competencies different from the past. This model helps achieve those particular skill sets and competencies.

We also believe that employee engagement not only holds the key to success but our survival as a robust US economy as well. To do so requires us to continuously evaluate things. The following model is how we believe employee engagement enables this to become a reality.

It takes work and there are no easy answers. In fact, taking the easy road has led us to less than stellar results as leaders. However, if this is followed, so will success. We don't have to complicate things. Our goal as leaders should be to simplify and make work life easier and more enjoyable. We need to break down barriers for us to have breakthrough performance.

If we want employee engagement (and most organizations do), then we have to have a plan to accomplish that very thing. The following model enables this to occur.

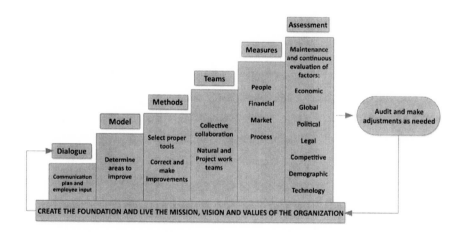

In this model, it should be noted that all we do organizationally begins with creating the foundation through our mission, vision, and values. Please note it is not enough to create them; we must live and embrace them daily.

We then embark on creating dialogue with our people, beginning with a communication plan which allows employee input. For too long, leadership has spoken the words but not lived up to them. What is your plan for communications? How do you touch employees each and every day?

In our normal course of work as consultants, we encounter organizations which throw something on a wall with the hope it sticks. This is a recipe for failure. To really make an impact, we must follow a model of improvement. Many consultants offer models of this sort and most of them work. We believe a model developed by Dr. Deming works fine, where we plan the work, do the work, study outcomes, and act upon them. Even if this means we did it wrong, what lessons did we learn? Not all things work the way we design them, but a model of improvement allows organizations to not repeat the same mistakes. There are no plausible reasons for continuing practices that don't fit. This is something that must stop and a model for improvement is a key to this.

We must also offer tools to employees to help them understand the nature of work and various interrelationships. This combined with a model for improvement actually empowers the workforce by creating buy-in and achievement. Management and leadership in general have too often used one tool: the hammer. Many years ago, it was understood that if the only tool we have is a hammer, it's no surprise all things start to resemble a nail.

In our chapter on myths and rituals, we explored the fact that a team is not a team in name only. To truly capture the essence of collaboration, we must provide training in how to work as a team in both a natural work team as well as project team setting. Accordingly, patience is required as teams go through learning together, but overall results are powerful and proven better than a person working alone.

We must also look at measuring things but not singularly through tabular results. We believe measures must be viewed in totality of the entire system and not just through financial reporting.

We tend to make the wrong decisions when singular data points are used as guides. We must look at a variety of measures, a true system of measures in order to make the right call. This means people, markets, financial *and* process measures.

We also need to make proper assessments. Assessments of economics, technology, and politics are just a few. When we attempt to make advances without exploring or assessing these items, the result oftentimes is waste. These are then audited in order to assure we are on the right path and make adjustments accordingly. This model is similar to the three pillars of an evolved workforce found in the previous chapter on discovery, development, and deployment.

We must do something significantly different from what we have been doing. Studies and insights indicate we are facing an uninspired workforce. This cannot lead to positive outcomes. For example, in a recent report prepared by Cornerstone, about nineteen million people left their jobs in 2013, costing upward of two trillion dollars in terms of employee churn. What makes an employee stay? There are very simple things leadership is able to do to make them feel appreciated, inclusive, and engaged. However, consider the following results which influence reasons people stay with their employer:

- 48 percent stay because they have a good manager.
- 46 percent feel they are appreciated.
- 39 percent stay for assumed job growth.
- 35 percent for recognition of achievements.
- 32 percent for the opportunity to develop new skills.

However, look at the numbers. Nothing cited indicates an approval of greater than 50 percent. This is even more exacerbated by the following results from the same survey.

- Only 30 percent received training and development to help them perform their jobs.
- Only 20 percent indicate reviews help them with attaining new skills which increase their performance.
- 13 percent of workers never receive any sort of feedback, and 60 percent of workers have not received any meaningful feedback in the previous six-month period.
- Only one in four employees has established career goals with their employers. Think about this. Only 25 percent of all workers have any career paths at a time when key skills are in demand.

We are not talking, and we are not developing. What a dismal report overall.

In conclusion, we have assimilated some key thoughts pertaining to leadership and its required transformation. A few were borrowed from elsewhere, and a few are of our own. The following items should become part of your daily reminders of what is required of leadership. In a small way, this is your path forward.

Leadership must remain resilient. Just keep swimming!

Leadership in General...

We are in a new economic age which requires a new set of competencies. Systems, variability, learning and living the vision are the skills leaders MUST possess.

Communications

Leaders must communicate well and communicate often with all stakeholders.

Spinning the truth will not achieve success. Communication needs to return to dialogue with people and be straightforward.

People/ relationships

Leaders should not attempt to control people. The system is usually what needs fixing, not people.

Leaders must develop relationships with suppliers, employees and customers. How each is treated impacts the end results.

Systems

Leaders must understand and apply skills to the system and understand the purpose behind key actions.

Leaders must understand the inter-relationships between departments, functions, divisions and the entire organization.

Carrots and sticks don't work. These are training tools for animals, not people.

The nature of work is changing. We are moving from a different set of skills and employee autonomy will be a factor in future success.

We need to question the efficacy of performance appraisal and why it needs to be done in the first place.

Teams

People must be taught to work together to achieve excellent results, in both natural and project team settings.

Leaders should avoid putting people to work on solving issues without training in problem resolution techniques.

A team isn't a team because people happen to work together.

Measures

Leaders must ask the right questions before establishing measures.

Measures must be reliable and offer predictability to be truly effective.

Leaders cannot rely on measures of the past to assure success in the future. Reliance on visible numbers such as financial reports alone cannot guide the organization.

Change

Change is constant.

Leader must look on the horizon to provide insight into direction.

Administrators do things right; leaders do the right thing.

Employ your people to help drive change.

Leaders must not succumb to the latest fads. They need a systematic method of handling change efforts.

False Assumptions

We must motivate people

We must hold people accountable for their actions

We must incentivize them to perform.

We must control.

References

Introduction

Mike Myatt, "The Most Misunderstood Aspect of Great Leadership." *Forbes. http://www.forbes.com/sites/mikemyatt/2012/12/26/the-most-misunderstood-aspect-of-great-leadership/* (August, 2103).

Gallup, "State of the American Workplace," "Employee Engagement Insights for U.S. Business Leaders." *http://www.gallup.com/strategicconsulting/163007/state-american-workplace.aspx* (June, 2013).

Kenexa, "Retail Sector at Risk through Lack of Engagement, New Study Claims." *http://www.kenexa.com/aboutkenexa/mediaroom/ctl/detail/mid/667/itemid/223* (February 21, 2012).

Peter Drucker, *The Eye of the Storm* (The Leadership Press, Inc., 1995).

Chapter 1

Warren Bennis, *On Becoming a Leader* (The Basic Book, 2009).

Wikipedia, "Maslow, Abraham." *http://en.wikipedia.org/wiki/Abraham_Maslow* (June, 2013).

Wikipedia, "Herzberg, Frederick." *http://en.wikipedia.org/wiki/Frederick_Herzberg* (June, 2013).

Wikipedia, "McGregor, Douglas." *http://en.wikipedia.org/wiki/Douglas_McGregor* (June, 2013).

Wikipedia, "Skinner, B. F." *http://en.wikipedia.org/wiki/B. F. Skinner* (June, 2013).

Ed. W. Deming, *Out of the Crisis* (The MIT Press, 1989).

Brainy Quotes, "Edison, Thomas." *http://www.brainyquote.com/quotes/authors/t/thomas_a_edison.html* (February, 2013).

Walter Isaacson, *Steve Jobs* (Simon & Schuster, 2011).

Fast Company, "Marcus Buckingham Thinks Your Boss Has an Attitude Problem." *http://www.fastcompany.com/43419/marcus-buckingham-thinks-your-boss-has-attitude-problem* (September, 2012).

Banff Centre, "The Leader as a Coach: Creating High Performance in Change." *http://www.banffcentre.ca/leadership/library/pdf/coach_22-24.pdf* (September, 2012).

Chapter 2

Cornerstone on Demand, "Empowering People." *http://www.cornerstoneondemand.com/news/press-releases/cornerstone-ondemand-survey-reveals-dramatic-skills-gap-within-american* (December 11, 2012).

Peter Scholtes, *The Leader's Handbook* (McGraw-Hill, 1999).

F. W. Taylor, *The Principles of Scientific Management* (Eldritch Press, 1911).

Wharton Speaks, Wharton School of Business, *"The Problem with Financial Incentives and What to Do about Them."* (March, 2011).

Reddit, "What Stupid Policies Does Your Current or Former Employer Have That You Don't Agree With?" *http://www.reddit. com/r/AskReddit/comments/13xhzj/what_stupid_policies_does_ your_current_or_former/* (February, 2013).

Ed. Deming, *"Quality, Productivity, and Competitive Position."* (Seminar, 1991).

Forbes, "Here's to the Death of Microsoft's Rank and Yank." *http:// www.forbes.com/sites/forbesleadershipforum/2013/11/13/heres- to-the-death-of-microsofts-rank-and-yank/* (November, 2013).

Brian Joiner (Brian Joiner and Associates), *The Team Handbook* (Pfeiffer, November, 1990).

George Garrett and Scott Playfair, (P2 Consulting), *Process Improvement Team Pocket Guide* (2000).

The Gallup Organization, "Gallup Survey of Employee Engagement." *http://www.gallup.com/strategicconsulting/164735/state-global- workplace.aspx* (September, 2013).

Society for Human Resources Management, "SHRM Workplace Forecast, The Top Workplace Trends According to HR Professionals." *http://www.shrm.org/research/futureworkplace trends/documents/13-0146%20workplace_forecast_full_fnl.pdf* (September, 2013).

Careerbliss, "50 Happiest Companies in America." *http://www. careerbliss.com/facts-and-figures/careerbliss-50-happiest- companies-in-america-for-2013/* (September, 2013).

TED Talks, Nancy Etcoff, PhD. (2009). *http://www.ted.com/ speakers/nancy_etcoff* (September, 2013).

Chapter 3

Peter Scholtes, *The Leader's Handbook* (McGraw-Hill, 1999).

Ed. Deming, *"Quality, Productivity, and Competitive Position."* (Seminar, 1991).

Brainy Quotes, "Kennedy, John F." http://www.brainyquote.com/quotes/authors/j/john_f_kennedy.html (February, 2013).

George Garrett and R. A. Long (Innova Management Consulting), *Linkage of Process* (Copyright, 2003).

Peter Senge, *The Fifth Discipline* (Doubleday/Currency, 1990).

Wikisource, "Saxe, John Godfrey." *http://en.wikisource.org/wiki/The_poems_of_John_Godfrey_Saxe/The_Blind_Men_and_the_Elephant* (February, 2014).

Chapter 4

Jane Logan, "Mission, Vision, Values," *Logan* Strategy. *http://www.loganstrategy.ca/content/articles/mission.pdf* (February, 2013).

Wikipedia, "Definition of Mission, Vision, and Values Statements." http://en.wikipedia.org/wiki/Strategic_planning (January, 2014).

Johnson & Johnson. http://www.jnj.com/sites/default/files/pdf/jnj_ourcredo_english_us_8.5x11_cmyk.pdf (February, 2014).

Starbucks, http://www.starbucks.com/ (February, 2014).

Veteran of Foreign Wars, http://www.vfw.org/Common/About-Us/ (February, 2014).

Special Olympics, http://www.specialolympics.mb.ca/aboutsom/mission-vision.php (February, 2014).

Novartis, http://www.novartis.com/careers/culture-values/index.shtml (February, 2014).

Bill George with Peter Sims, *True North. Discover Your Authentic Leadership* (Jossey-Bass, 2007).

Chapter 5

Daniel H. Pink, *Drive: The Surprising Truth About What Motivates Us* (Riverhead Books, 2009).

Society of Human Resources Management, "The Truth about the Upcoming Labor Shortage." *http://www.shrm.org/Publications/hrmagazine/EditorialContent/Pages/0305covstory.aspx* (March, 2005).

US Department of Labor (2005), "The United States Population Is Becoming Larger and More Diverse." *www.dol.gov* (February, 2014).

US Census Bureau (2002), "Baby Bust: US Births at Record Low." *http://money.cnn.com/2013/09/06/news/economy/birth-rate-low/* (April, 2014).

Chapter 6

John Childress & Larry Senn, *In the Eye of the Storm* (Leadership Press, 1995).

Search for Common Ground, *https://www.sfcg.org/?gclid=CNuGlc CcssACFZBAMgodEjcAfA* (January, 2014).

WBI: The Workplace Bullying Institute, "Being Bullied? Start Here." *http://www.workplacebullying.org/individuals/problem/ being-bullied/* (April, 2014).

New York Post "Gossip's Nearly All the Buzz" (December 9, 2012). *http://nypost.com/2012/12/09/gossips-nearly-all-the-buzz/* (April, 2014).

Chapter 7

Wikipedia, "Duell, Charles H." *http://en.wikipedia.org/wiki/ Charles_Holland_Duell* (November, 2013).

Rinkworks, "Things People Said." *http://www.rinkworks.com/ said/* (November, 2013).

Wikipedia, Richard Beckhard and David Gleicher, "Formula for Change, Organization Development: Strategies and Models" (1969). *http://en.wikipedia.org/wiki/Formula_for_Change* (November, 2013).

The Gallup Organization "Gallup Survey of Employee Engagement." *http://www.gallup.com/strategicconsulting/164735/state-global-workplace.aspx* (November, 2013).

Congregational Development, "The Change Formula." *http://www. congregationaldevelopment.com/storage/Change%20formula.pdf* (February, 2014).

Michael Beer and Nina Nohria, "Cracking the Code of Change," *Harvard Business Review* (May, 2000). *http://www.iesep.com/ en/cracking-the-code-of-change-harvard-business-review- article-37573.html (November, 2013).*

Wikipedia, "Kübler-Ross model, On Death and Dying." *http:// en.wikipedia.org/wiki/K%C3%BCbler-Ross model* (January, 2014).

Thomas Kuhn, *The Structure of Scientific Revolutions* (University of Chicago Press, 1962)

Joel Barker, *The Business of Discovering the Future* (HarperReprint, 1993).

Chapter 8

Motivational Quotes, "Moore, Thomas." *http://www.motivational quotes.com/pages/education-quotes.html* (January, 2014).

Forbes. "Seven Ways to Inspire Employees to Love Their Jobs." http://www.forbes.com/sites/carminegallo/2013/06/21/seven- ways-to-inspire-employees-to-love-their-jobs/ (June, 2013).

George Garrett and Theresa Zimmermann, Future Focus Group, *Pillars of an Evolved Workforce. http://futurefocusgroup.com/* (Copyrighted, 2013).

Globoforce Limited, "The Science of Happiness. How to Build a Killer Culture in Your Company." (Whitepaper) *http://www.usgs.gov/*

humancapital/ecd/mentoringreadinglist/Science of Happiness. pdf (January, 2014).

Itner and Douds, *Train the Trainer* (Human Resource Development Press, 2nd Edition, 1997).

Future Focus Group, LLC., "The Employee Development System." *http://futurefocusgroup.com/* (Copyright, 2013).

Jessica Pryce-Jones, "Ways to Be Happy and Productive at Work." *http://blogs.wsj.com/source/2012/11/25/five-ways-to-be-happy-and-productive-at-work/* (November 25, 2012).

Chapter 9

US Bureau of Labor Statistics, "U6 Unemployment Data." *http://www.bls.gov/* (January, 2014).

Reason.com, "Dirty Jobs' Mike Rowe on the High Cost of College." *http://reason.com/reasontv/2013/12/13/dirty-jobs-mike-rowe-on-the-high-cost-of* (December, 2013).

Wikipedia, "Mondragon." *http://en.wikipedia.org/wiki/Mondragon Corporation* (December, 2013).

Wikipedia, "B Corporations." *http://en.wikipedia.org/wiki/Benefit corporation* (December, 2013).

Wikipedia, "Low Profit, Limited Liability Corporations (L3C)." *http://en.wikipedia.org/wiki/Low-profit limited liability company* (December, 2013).

Chapter 10

Walt Disney Pictures, Pixar Animation Studios, *Finding Nemo*. (Buena Vista Pictures, 2003).

Future Focus Group, LLC., "Leadership System." *http://future focusgroup.com/* (2013).

Cornerstone on Demand, "Empowering People." *http://www. cornerstoneondemand.com/news/press-releases/cornerstone-ondemand-survey-reveals-dramatic-skills-gap-within-american* (December 11, 2012).

George Garrett

George Garrett is a founding member of Future Focus Group, LLC. He has spent his career in the field of human resources and continuous improvement consulting.

George resides in Texas.

Theresa Zimmermann

Theresa Zimmermann is a founding member of Future Focus Group. She spent most of her career in the medical services field.

Theresa resides in Wisconsin.

Future Focus Group, LLC specializes in helping small to mid-sized organizations improve leadership, strategy, and operating systems.

CPSIA information can be obtained at www.ICGtesting.com
Printed in the USA
LVOW08*1144251014

410462LV00002B/7/P